MANGAN'S
WAR

Frank Mangan

✳ ✳ ✳ ✳ ✳
KEEP THOSE LETTERS

MRS. W. C. ROCHE, 1515 Hardaway, is putting letters from her son, Sgt. Frank Mangan, in bound form and will keep them for him to read in the years to come. Sergeant Mangan tells a story in each of his letters. He has been in various parts of Europe and his letters are very descriptive.

That would be a good idea for other mothers to adopt. Some day, they or their sons would like very much to read those letters again. If they are placed chronologically in a bound file, they will be easy to keep and easy to follow.

✳ ✳ ✳ ✳ ✳

MANGAN'S WAR

A Personal View of World War II

— BY —

FRANK J. MANGAN

MANGAN BOOKS

El Paso, Texas

Published by Mangan Books
6245 Snowheights Court, El Paso, Texas 79912

Printed in the United States of America

Library of Congress Cataloging-in-Publication Data

Mangan, Frank J.
    Mangan's war / Frank John Mangan – 1st ed.
        p. cm.
    Includes bibliographical references and index.
    ISBN 0-930208-39-0
    1. Mangan, Frank J. 2. World War, 1939-1945—Personal
narratives, American. 3. World War, 1939-1945—Campaigns—
Western Front. 4. United States. Army Air Forces—Biogra-
phy. I. Title.
D811.M3346A3 2003
940.54'21'092—dc21
[B]

                                        2003051341

10   9   8   7   6   5   4   3   2   1

To Judy

*—whose writing and editing
talents are spread liberally
throughout this book.*

BOOKS BY FRANK J. MANGAN

Bordertown

El Paso in Pictures

Bordertown Revisited

The Pipeliners

Ruidoso Country

Mangan's War

Contents

Foreword

THROUGH THE YEARS, I've noticed that life for me is neatly divided into two chunks, before The War and after The War. World War II was "The War." It was the biggest. It was the bloodiest in the world's history. Thousand-plane Allied air raids over Germany were the norm rather than the unusual. In June 1944 America and her allies launched the mighty amphibious invasion of Normandy, the largest the world had ever seen. By 1945 three million men and women were fighting Germany under General Dwight D. Eisenhower. Civilians died by the millions. Germans alone killed six million Jews in the Holocaust. European cities were not only smashed, many were obliterated. Hiroshima, Japan almost disappeared when an American B-29 dropped one bomb. My heartfelt thanks to Harry Truman.

This story is gleaned from letters I wrote to my mother and other family members during World War II from 1942 to 1945. My mother saved them in thick loose-leaf notebooks and gave them to me years later. I read them again in 1985. My wife Judy wanted to preserve the letters and she converted them to type on her computer. After looking over this collection I saw lots of incidents that needed further explaining. In many spots my memory is blurred by time but I have ransacked my brain to pull it all together. So this is a memoir.

From overseas, letters were heavily censored. You couldn't tell anybody where you were other than saying, for instance, somewhere in France—or England—or Germany. You couldn't mention combat or enemy action. Consequently many of the letters were pretty well restricted to comments about the weather, the food or lack of it, or just general griping and telling the folks back home how much you missed them.

For most of us the 1940s were simpler times. We were patriotic. In this war America had been attacked and all of us, at home or abroad, were involved. Unlike the later Korean and Vietnam wars, servicemen and women in World War II had full backing on the home front. Anti-war protests were unheard of. America's giant war factories hummed twenty-four hours a day sending war materials to the military, which spread across much of the world.

Women were taking over men's jobs while men were in the service. These women helped make airplanes, ships, tanks, ammunition, and hundreds of other war-related products, all on jobs that were previously held by men. They donned men's denim overalls since there was no such thing as work clothes for women in the early years of the war. But it wasn't long before clothing stores caught up with the denim demand. And Rosie the Riveter became the symbol of America's women factory workers.

Ranging from teenagers to middle age these women received nationwide acclaim. In 1943 Rosie the Riveter appeared on a *Saturday Evening Post* cover by Norman Rockwell. My future sister-in-law, Patty Peterson Gilbert, became one of those riveters on B-17s at the huge Lockheed plant in Burbank, California. In the nation's shipyards they and their male counterparts cranked

Rosie the Riveter, a famous Saturday Evening Post cover by Norman Rockwell, became the symbol of America's women factory workers after Pearl Harbor. Thousands of women took over men's jobs while men were in the service.

out a giant Liberty ship every sixty days. These ships were considerably longer than a football field and could carry as many as 230 million rounds of ammunition from America to our Allies in Europe. The Axis Powers were ultimately overwhelmed with America's ability to produce arms. Americans got by on strict rationing. No ration stamp, no new shoes. No ration stamp, no meat. No ration stamp, no gasoline. Three gallons a week was the ration for "non-essential drivers." Civilians knew a war was going on and they wanted to do their part. They planted Victory Gardens in their back yards and vacant lots and grew vegetables for their dinner tables. They saved tin cans, string, paper, tinfoil, anything that could be consumed by the war effort. I still wonder why they saved string.

In spite of home front backing and personal patriotism, as GIs (that means Government Issue) we griped about the military and the System—but not about America. We complained about the food and weather everywhere. Each new location seemed worse than the last. We grumbled constantly about regimentation and taking really dumb orders from others who may have been in the service only a few months longer than we were.

Some of those days were traumatic, some were merely hectic, but they were all memorable. I enjoyed reading those old letters. They recalled experiences I hadn't thought about for decades.

C Rations, anyone?

*S*OME YEARS AGO *I was assisting General James Polk collect some random thoughts for his memoirs of World War II. We ran across the speech delivered by General George S. Patton to his troops in May 1944 shortly before the Normandy invasion. I think these last three paragraphs say a lot about The War.*

—Frank Mangan
El Paso, Texas 2003

ॐ

REMEMBER, MEN, you don't know I'm here. No mention of that is to be made in any letters. The USA is supposed to be wondering what the hell has happened to me. I'm not supposed to be commanding this army. I'm not supposed even to be in England. Let the first bastards to find out be the goddamn Germans. I want them to look up and howl, "Ach, it's the goddamn Third Army and that son of a bitch Patton again!"

We want to get this thing over and get the hell out of here, and get at those purple-pissin' Japs! The shortest road home is through Berlin and Tokyo! We'll win this war, but we'll win it only by showing the enemy that we have more guts than they have or ever will have!

There's one great thing you men can say when it's all over and you're home once more. You can thank God that twenty years from now, when you're sitting around the fireside with your grandson on your knee and he asks what you did in the war, you won't have to shift him to the other knee, cough, and say, "I shoveled shit in Louisiana."

MANGAN'S
WAR

1

Just Lucky, I Guess

THERE WERE ONLY THREE possible assignments that appealed to me during World War II. I would have liked being on the staff of *The Stars and Stripes*. After I finished the U.S. Army Air Corps Photo School, I looked forward to becoming an aerial photographer flying in B-17s and B-24s. My third interest was to become a lieutenant instead of a private. This item was last on the list and the only reason it even made third was that my mother wished so hard for it. Fortunately, as things worked out, none of the above happened. It turns out I was just plain lucky through the whole war. And I think my luck began at a dreary Air Corps boot camp in Kearns, Utah in October 1942. I remember the shower facilities were still open air in this unfinished camp on a frigid wind swept prairie. It was weird there doing close order drill carrying wooden guns made out of 2 x 4s and firing wooden machine guns because of the nation's shortage of arms and ammunition.

Most Americans had no idea how ill prepared the army was

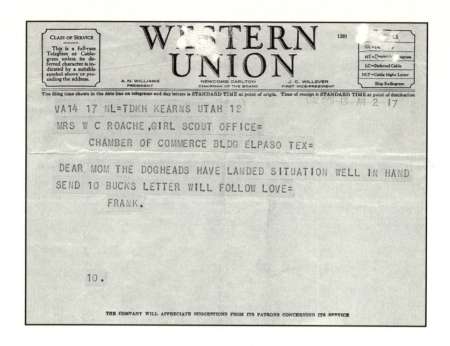

when we went to war. I know I didn't—until I got to Utah. When Germany marched into Poland starting World War II in 1939 our army's enlisted strength in the United States was less than 130,000. My entire basic training lasted less than two weeks, and I never saw one of those gruff drill sergeants that are depicted on today's TV. But after ROTC in high school, I already knew that stuff. At least in high school we drilled with Springfield rifles; although most of our uniforms were army surplus from World War I, wrapped leggings and all. Did I mention that I was a draftee? Well I was. And the Army wanted us recruits overseas as quickly as possible—even without much basic training.

That's how I got to Lowry Field in Denver so quickly. Lowry was the home of the Army Air Corps Photo School. And I think management selected me because I bragged to somebody that I knew how to develop Box Brownie film. The course lasted three months, with an emphasis on shooting photos from heavy bombers. Our class pictures showed us wearing fleece lined leather bomber jackets and headphones. While we waited to ship out after graduation they moved 1,500 of us into temporary quarters in a huge new barracks, supposedly the largest brick barracks in the world. It covered several square blocks, four stories high. They said a person could live there for a lifetime and never leave the building. A mess hall, movie theater, post office, tailor shop, cleaners, laundry, Post Exchange, pool hall, bowling alley, and a library occupied one floor. I slept in the same room with 350 other guys who either snored or rolled dice all night. Twenty radios tuned to different stations blared constantly. Sheer bedlam.

Within a week the entire (almost) group of photo graduates shipped out to various air bases. I missed the shipment. Seems they lost my name and I simply vanished from the records. I asked the sergeant what to do and he told me to just sit tight and don't move till I heard from him. That was the last time I saw him. So here I was, living in sheer luxury in a huge brick barracks, one floor to myself. I strolled down to the mess hall at civilized times instead of those impossible middle-of-the-night breakfasts on the graveyard shift at school. Nobody bothered me or asked any stupid questions. I figured I would just stay put, wait out the war, never get shot at or pull KP or pick up any more cigarette butts. There WAS a God!

I would sleep till noon, eat a good lunch in the mess hall, hang around the PX, go outside and watch it snow and then go to the movies. Such a deal. Happiest guy in the U.S. Army. But realism set in. Who was gonna pay me my fifty dollars a month? Also that huge room looked bigger and emptier every day. I even began to miss the ambient sound of radio music. So I got patriotic and turned myself in. The Head Office was unbelievably cordial, simply because this whole little glitch was their fault. They knew it and they knew I knew it. So they happily shipped me out with the next graduating class. Getting Mangan out of there quietly

3

was like getting rid of smallpox. They breathed a sigh of relief and I was on a troop train heading east. Incidentally, that brick barracks would be the last place in three years where I would eat a hot meal from anything but a mess kit.

The temperature was below zero when I left Denver on a troop train. About the third day out we pulled into Evansville, Indiana and were greeted by several hundred cheery citizens who handed us sandwiches, cookies, coffee, donuts and other goodies. I'll always have a warm spot in my heart for patriotic Evansville, Indiana.

I woke up in the morning of the fifth day and glanced out the train window at Orlando, Florida and two girls in tennis shorts. I debarked wearing one of those heavy ankle-length horse blanket overcoats. The temperature was eighty degrees. The date was February 4, 1943 and I could hardly believe my newest stroke of luck.

2

Zephyrhills—Back to the Thirties

About an hour's truck ride west of Orlando the tiny town of Zephyrhills dozed in the central Florida orange groves. It was the highest point in Florida (ten feet, I think) and base of the 10th Fighter Squadron. This was to be my new home, and it was not unattractive. Another GI and I from Lowry Field Photo School checked in with the first sergeant. He asked me what we were doing in his fighter squadron. "Well, this is where they sent us." The other guy was named Thomas Mansell and no matter where I went, there was Mansell because both our names started with Man. The sergeant told us they didn't have cameras there and had no occasion to use photography. So we could become mechanics, or armorers or cooks/bakers or pull general duty. We both chose to be armorers, whatever they were. I couldn't get rid of Mansell.

But becoming an armorer wasn't all that bad. Within a few days I could remove .50 caliber machine guns from the wings of Curtis P-40 Warhawk fighter planes, take them apart, clean them and put them back without any parts left over. The 10th was a pre-war outfit that flew P-35 airplanes before they received the new P-40s. You could tell the enlisted men weren't new to the army because all their fatigue uniforms had that great faded green and lived-in look. Whereas Mansell and I stood out like the raw recruits we were in our stiff new dark green fatigues.

The hell of it was that nearly all my new found companions were already staff sergeants—at a minimum, and since non-coms were excused from KP, latrines, garbage and other crummy jobs, guess who pulled all these so-called "shit details?" (This was the affectionate term used throughout the U.S. Armed Forces.) For a time I lived in sort of a return to the 1930s atmosphere. When I ran short of fatigues, the supply sergeant issued me a blue floppy hat and a blue jumper, matching the El Paso Levis I wore most of the time—like you used to see in the old pre-war army. It was pretty casual around there and nobody seemed to give a damn what I wore. Our supply sergeant still sported a Smokey Bear hat with a stiff brim. Had they ever heard of Pearl Harbor around here?

Since this was all new to the citizens of Zephyrhills and they had seldom seen doggies the likes of us, they let us date their pretty daughters and drive their Model A Fords. The Cherry family invited me to dinner every Sunday. Of course, the fried chicken always tasted a bit like kerosene because that's what they cooked with. It was a real treat to get away from army food once a week. These people were the warmest, friendliest folks I'd ever run into, and nearly all the old GIs from the 10th will happily tell you that little Zephyrhills was the best place we were ever stationed. The town had one main street and it was named Fifth Avenue. Large trees in a center island provided cool, dappled shade. There was the two-story Zephyr Hotel with a wooden porch that wrapped around the second floor. Newcomb's Drugstore had a real soda fountain and ice cream chairs, in use long before this décor became quaint. Their specialty was twenty-five cent banana splits with huge scoops of vanilla, chocolate and strawberry ice cream topped off with the appropriate syrups, whipped cream, nuts and a cherry. And at the end of the block was the First Baptist Church. One Sunday the church sent word to the airbase that after services in the evening there would be cookies and punch for the GIs. So a buddy of mine, Private Phil Pearce and I cleaned up and went to church. We suffered through the sermon and then sought out the cookies. Four really nice church ladies greeted us and poured punch. It turned out to be pretty embarrassing because we were the only soldiers who showed up. After what seemed like hours we left and headed back to the base, only about a mile away.

Zephyrhills had a population of about 1,000 with several roadside places that served beer, well removed from town. These beer joints strung out along the highway were not merely sleazy, some were absolutely dangerous. One, called Purdy's Hawaiian Inn, had a ratty fake palm tree or two and produced, on a quite predictable basis, Saturday night fights with broken beer bottles and knives. Some dreadfully drunk civilians who were probably nervous that their local women were being taken over by the GIs usually provoked these. The GI contingent also had its share of belligerents, mostly roughnecks from the oil fields of Texas and Oklahoma who didn't back off when the fighting started.

Another establishment, simply sleazy and not always dangerous, was called Mom's. (There is always a Mom's in most towns.) Mom was a white haired lady of probably sixty, who was absolutely dippy over a squadron cook, a much younger guy named Francis Xavier Hill. He was one of the former Texas roughnecks —and one mean son of a bitch. It was very handy for Mom, who was a nice, friendly lady. She had Sergeant Hill in the sack, and he also cooked hamburgers for the customers while Mom poured the beer. Not a bad setup if you think about it.

7

In the entire complex of town-plus-airbase there were few telephones. One in our operations building, another in the City Hall, and a few more scattered around the citrus groves. There was a certain amount of charm in being in a town so un-hustled, so unlike the twentieth century. It seemed to me every man drove a Model A Ford. I didn't see many women drivers but I guess they were at home doing what women were supposed to do in those times. I'm pretty sure Zephyrhills was like the Elephants' Graveyard. All Model A Fords went there to die.

The nice thing about being stationed in Zephyrhills was that while other GIs around the country were doing all the usual things GIs had to do, we were exempt from military spit and polish or regulations. Thanks to the squadron commander, twenty-six-year-old Major George Kiser, who simply didn't believe in the rulebook. He had recently returned from the Pacific where he became America's No. 2 Ace—flying P-40s against the Japanese. So we were proud to have him as our commanding officer. His philosophy was "You keep the planes in shape to do their flying and bombing and I'll handle the rest of the stuff." A very refreshing attitude in the regulation-heavy U.S. Armed Forces, and how he got away with it I don't know. So the planes were kept in shape, and then as darkness approached in the evenings we were off on the mile walk into town. No passes needed as I recall, no signing in or out, no nothing. The major seemed secure in his belief that the purpose of the Air Corps was to fly planes, and that meant they be maintained and armed perfectly. The purpose was not to make beds with perfect corners, stand inspections, have parades, polish brass belt buckles, shine shoes, or any of the other things that were a civilian's idea of what war was all about. Of course, some of my close New Army buddies and I spent an inordinate amount of time on KP. Somebody had to do it and it always fell to the new guys. To this day, I still don't know how to make up a bed and I hate cleaning a kitchen.

The girls in Zephyrhills were mostly pretty and really nice, in a charming southern sort of way. There just weren't enough to go around but it worked out. Every Saturday night they had a dance for us in the Legion Hall (where else?). They had a Wurlitzer jukebox that furnished all the current music—like "Pistol Packin' Mama," "Stardust," "You'll Never Know," all the wartime big band sounds. Strangely though, as I look back, nobody was jitterbugging. I certainly didn't know how. But we were sort of hidden back in the palmettos. There were a few romances, some light, some heavy. Doris Cherry wrote to me faithfully all during the war. This whole experience seemed like something right out of a pleasant "Twilight Zone." The girls—and their parents as well—were what they called "Crackers" (their words) as in Georgia Crackers. I don't think any of them had ever been to places like Miami. But then neither had I.

In spite of cleaning out grease traps and latrines, I wound up with a perfect deal when summer arrived. The town had a nice swimming pool, but with the war on, there was nobody to run it and keep drownings to a minimum. The first sergeant asked me and another guy if we'd be interested in life guarding and chlorinating the pool every afternoon until suppertime. No problemo! But first we had to journey to Orlando every day for two weeks, swim in a lake with about fifty other swimmers (some were Olympic swimmers—tough competition). Most of us got our Red Cross Water Safety Instructors credentials. We would then teach other GIs Senior Life Saving. We also taught soldiers what to do should their troop ship get torpedoed on the way to the war. This was really fun. We had a thirty-foot wooden platform out in the lake. Infantry troops from around Orlando would come in loaded down with full packs. We'd coax these poor bastards to the top of the platform, ignite the lake water with gasoline, and push them off yelling. Nobody drowned and it was actually good training. And I got out of cleaning machine guns and garbage cans.

9

Back in Zephyrhills on Sunday afternoons a few of us would draw rifles and ammunition, then go tramping around in the pine/palmetto woods and shoot at anything that moved. But all was not Sunday on the farm. Shit details stretched on month after month, and the best of the lot was latrine duty. You cleaned the toilets and shower room in your barracks which were newly built tarpaper and wood buildings. The army brass in Washington obviously figured it would take one GI a full day to scrub a dozen toilets, clean and disinfect the shower room, and keep the coal-burning furnace in the boiler room from going out. I got so good at this I could do the whole day's work in two hours, and then hide out the rest of the day while the war droned on. The best deal by far on KP was working Officers Mess. I would stand behind the tables with my arms crossed until somebody ran out of, say, potatoes. Then I'd fill his plate. Some of my buddies sort of resented this duty as being too subservient, but I accepted it because it wasn't messy like cleaning grease traps. And besides, I had a ton of respect for those fighter pilots.

As you can imagine, central Florida with its low altitude, high humidity, and water, water everywhere attracted every bug in the Free World. Worst of all were the bedbugs, which descended like locusts on any warm body. We slept on these typical canvas army cots and the damn bugs loved to make babies where the canvas and the wooden parts joined together. In desperation, we bought out the town's supply of blowtorches, and every couple of days we'd haul all the cots outside and cook bedbugs. Probably shortened the war by at least a year.

The 10th Fighter Squadron was one of three which comprised the 50th Fighter Group. The others, the 81st and 313th were based nearby at similar fields. The 81st was at Cross City and the 313th was at Leesburg. After the then obsolete P-40s were phased out we became a P-51 Mustang outfit. And everybody liked the change to the new, faster P-51. The squadron consisted

My fatigue uniform consisted of a pre-Pearl Harbor blue denim jumper, blue floppy hat, and civilian Levis sent from home. I was able to mop and clean the barracks in about two hours, then hide out the rest of the day while the war droned on.

of 38 officers (mostly pilots) and 252 enlisted men. Several nights a week, in an effort to keep the troops' morale up, we would have movies under the trees. The squadron owned a 16-millimeter projector, and since I was supposed to be a photographer, who would be more logical to become the projectionist? Me, of course. I didn't mind it except whenever the film broke, the audience (seated on the ground) would jeer and direct ingenious obscenities at me until I could get the damn show going again. But the brass surprised me one day by making me a PFC—Private First Class. My pals thought it was wonderful so they held me down and painted single stripes on the sleeves of my blue jumper.

Little did they know I got a payday increase of $4.00 so I was now drawing $54 each and every month. Not too bad.

The 10th remained intact as a squadron, which was very unusual. The customary procedure was to break up stateside outfits and start new ones and then ship the personnel out to whatever part of the world needed some bodies. The tough part of going out as replacements meant getting re-assigned into God knows what kind of outfit, and not having any friends. It meant being a newcomer all over again.

But we remained intact for the best part of three years and got to know and be friends with just about everybody. Except one, and that happened to be the aforementioned Sergeant Francis X. Hill. "Meaner'n a snake" they called him. One little incident took place in Hill's mess hall shortly before we shipped out of Zephyrhills. I'd been working in the kitchen with another kid who suddenly got sick and headed rapidly for the barracks. Hill came storming up (pretty drunk) and accused me of leaving an open ketchup bottle on a table. I explained that the other kid went on sick call and couldn't wait to clean off his last table. But Hill shouted, "three days extra duty!" Another KP, a tall drink of water from Harlan County, Kentucky then stepped up to enter the shouting match. I can't remember his name but he was fresh out of a hidden hollow somewhere deep in the mountains of Appalachia, where paved roads were still a myth. Like many of his peers he was built like a middle linebacker, with blond hair and light gray eyes (caused, they used to say, by everybody marrying their cousin). He confronted Hill and quietly told him that I didn't deserve the extra three days. The sergeant got livid and his red-purple face fumed. He shouted, "Get out of here, you son of a bitch!" With that, my Kentucky pal got real serious and said, "If you ever call my mother a dirty name again I'll kill you." One of Hill's cooks heard that and said, "Sergeant, he really will kill you. Let's just walk away." Well, that defused the mess hall confrontation and I walked over to the first sergeant's office in the orderly room and called foul (planning to go through the chain of command). He told me there wasn't anything he could change and that I should do the three days and then forget it. I did the extra time but I never forgot it.

Back to the real war. It was time to go, and early in March 1944 the 10th, as well as the two other fighter squadrons in the 50th Group started packing. Within several hours the whole civilian population of Zephyrhills heard the news and the next few days saw lots of hugs, teary kisses and handshakes. According to some local folks, another fighter squadron, the 9th, had been there earlier. They were supposedly shipped to Christmas Island in the Pacific, overrun by the Japanese and all killed. The Zephyrhills civilians didn't want us to suffer the same bad luck overseas. And neither did we.

We convoyed over to Orlando Air Base and moved into barracks with double bunks. Everybody wanted to get a top bunk, as did I. Turned out to be one of my major mistakes, as I discovered the first night. The ceiling was only about four or five feet above the top bunks and at night what I perceived as a dark brown ceiling was actually solid cockroaches. Millions of them had come out of the woodwork and were walking upside down on the ceiling. I just lay there in darkness, scared that the damn roaches would start falling on me any minute. But they didn't. Actually, they proved to be better bedfellows than the bedbugs in Zephyrhills. It was just the idea that drove me nuts. I figured Real War couldn't be this scary.

But life goes on. The supply depot issued all the necessary equipment to keep from getting killed or maimed overseas. We, of course, still didn't have the foggiest idea where we'd be going. But hoped it would be Europe and not some hellhole in southern New Guinea. Most of us got .30 caliber carbines complete with three 15 round clips of ammunition. Some non-coms got

Thompson sub-machine guns and the pilots and other officers got .45-caliber automatic pistols. We really liked the carbines, especially those made by the Winchester Repeating Arms Company (I got one of these and was real pleased because Winchester carried such a John Wayne reputation). Some of the other GIs were handed carbines made by a number of different companies like Singer or Wurlitzer. One guy started complaining and his buddy said, "Aw, shut up. Wurlitzer makes a damn good juke box."

3

Hard Way to Get to a War

In the middle of March 1944 we climbed aboard a troop train and headed up the East Coast. By now we were convinced our destination was someplace in England. And for once nobody complained. The port of embarkation was Camp Shanks, New York. In the middle of the night, after a week at Camp Shanks, we boarded an old British ocean liner, our home for the next two weeks. I swear I could almost hear the fifes and drums playing "Yankee Doodle Dandy" as we struggled up the gangplank with all our possessions on our backs. At least I figured an Army band would play "Stars and Stripes Forever" for such an occasion. But no, it was "Pistol Packin' Mama" followed by "Papa's off to the Seven Seas." This troop ship was a real tub. Its name was HMS *Stirling Castle,* converted to hold six thousand troops packed into every available inch. For what it's worth, we were part of the largest convoy to ever cross the Atlantic.

The sleeping arrangements were nothing like you had seen in the movies, with bunks stacked about five deep. Old *Stirling*

Castle, also known to the troops as Starving Castle, did have a bunch of these, but it also had troops sleeping on the floor, on top of mess hall tables, and the worst place of all, a big empty swimming pool. Naturally, that's where I was assigned. Everybody picked up hammocks from one end of the pool and stretched them between hooks mounted on wooden poles. There were hundreds of them and every hammock touched every other one, so you always had at least two sets of feet in your face. There was no way you could lie on your side without falling to the floor. Naturally, everybody slept in their uniforms. What drove me nuts was the visual nightmare of swinging slowly back and forth in the hammock while the ship rolled. My eyes played tricks on my brain as I watched the floor slanting from two feet at one end to eight feet at the other. As if this weren't bizarre enough, the creaking and groaning of the ship's timbers assaulted my ears. A little scary. You really began to wonder if this boat would make it all the way to England.

I'd always had a tendency to get nauseated—even on merry-go-rounds, so this cruise was destined to take its toll on me. I got sick before the ship left the dock, and I wasn't alone, thank God. The second night out was the worst and the waves got larger as we plowed into the North Atlantic. At six in the morning, a sergeant started blowing a whistle for all of the hammock guys to get up. They rolled up their hammocks and got in line for what the British laughingly called breakfast. Everybody got up but me. I had been throwing up all night—too weak to stand. So I just froze where I was. Then I got the first of three ranking visitors. I figured they would probably extend some sympathy and get me to the ship's hospital. This first guy was a tech sergeant, very big, very mean, and obviously figured the word "sympathy" could be found in the dictionary between "shit" and "syphilis." He growled, "Okay, soldier, on your feet and get in line or you're in big trouble." I merely shook my head, closed my eyes and turned over. After muttering a few obscenities at me, he did an about face and stormed off to bring in some more muscle.

My next visitor was a clean cut, no nonsense lieutenant. In an agitated voice he told me that if I continued to disobey and didn't get up he could actually recommend a court martial and I would be in real big trouble. I didn't know anything about military law but I had to assume he wasn't kidding. However, I stayed put and whispered grimly (and not really smart ass) to go ahead with plans for a court martial, execute me and put me out of this misery. He just shook his head and walked out of the swimming pool.

I covered my head with the blanket so I couldn't see the inside of the dizzying empty room. Then I heard a calm voice say, "You got a problem, son?" I peeked up at a rather friendly looking officer with gold oak leaves on his shirt—a major. I said, "Yes sir, I'm sicker than hell on this boat and I've had the dry heaves for two days and I can't stand up." The major asked, "What have you been eating?" I told him, "Nothing for two days but I can't stand the thought of runny scrambled eggs and boiled fish heads." This comment (which was true) struck a chord with him and he told me he'd be right back, and walked briskly up to the shallow end of the pool—and out. In about five minutes back he came carrying three khaki-colored tins of British field rations. The contents looked like American biscuits frozen in time. But he called them hardtack. I was certain then and still am today that these biscuits were left over from World War I. Even the printing on the cans looked old-timey. But I wasn't bargaining from a position of strength. I needed all the help I could get. The major wasn't a doctor but he had obviously been on lots of ships in the army. He looked me straight in the eye and said, "Your problem is that you don't have anything in your stomach and you're gonna get sicker every hour until you have something to throw up. He then agreed with me that the ship's food was pretty bad but to go ahead and gnaw on one of these biscuits right away. I was like a dog chewing on a bone, but indeed I got the first morsel down—and it stayed there.

I felt a little better immediately and promised this wonderful father-figure that I would get up after he told me where to get more hardtack. This gentle soul had literally saved a life. I managed to struggle out of the damn hammock and stagger out to the deck inhaling a huge breath of icy fresh air. I had survived. Some guys never did get sick but there were hundreds heaving all over the place trying to make it to the garbage cans to throw up in. The smell below decks was so bad I spent as much time as I could on deck. It was freezing cold and windy and rainy but I could breathe, even though the sky was dark gray and sea was black. On the stormier days of this little cruise the waves were over fifty feet high—like five story buildings.

But I continued surviving on British hardtack, and I even got in the chow line where they fed the GIs twice a day—breakfast and supper. Everybody stood up to eat on long, narrow wooden chest-high boards. They said this would keep your mess kit from sliding away. I still couldn't stand the smell of food but was able to get lots of bread (and it was pretty good. I guess bread worldwide is pretty good). Once in a while they gave us an apple, so I did okay. I figured they must have lots of apples stored somewhere, so two buddies and I made a stealthy trip into the bowels of the ship. Sure enough, there were boxes of American apples stacked to the ceiling. The three of us lugged a wooden box of those beautiful apples up hundreds of metal stairs and only ran afoul of one Englishman. We told him to get the hell out of the way or we would have to kill him. So he decided "what the hell" and kept walking down the stairs looking over his shoulder at our backs as we continued briskly on up to comparative safety. We kept as many apples as we could and handed out the rest to other starving GIs. With good bread and those apples I survived the trip. One kid in our outfit got so sick they were forced to hospitalize him and feed him intravenously all the way across. I made it but lost fifteen pounds during those two miserable weeks in the convoy. But who needed to lose fifteen pounds at that tender age?

We sighted land the first week in April 1944 and disembarked at Liverpool, England, down that wonderful gangplank and onto the lovely dry land of England. I've loved the British ever since just for being there and greeting all six thousand Americans as we thankfully came ashore. I still can't say anything nice about their boats.

In no time at all our 50th Fighter Group got sorted out and marched to the nearby rail yards where we boarded a rather charming (really) bunch of day coaches. The English country-side rolled by swiftly outside the windows as we headed due south from northern Liverpool to the southern Channel coast of Hampshire, near the Isle of Wight. We were in for some sur-prises, though. I thought we'd be assigned to the American Eighth Air Force, living in Quonset huts on a large airbase. But it was not to be—and just as well. Our field was merely a landing strip carved out of one of England's oldest estates, near the village of Lymington. Our steel mesh runway ran right by the front door of a stately mansion owned by an English lord named Pylewell. We were now in the Ninth Air Force whose mission was to provide support for the infantry and tank divisions, as well as low level strafing and dive-bombing. It took only about a minute to under-stand that we would be living in pup tents, and not nice warm Quonset huts. After that boat ride, any port in a storm.

But we were in for a pleasant surprise. Our commanding of-ficer, Major Kiser, had arrived several days earlier and awaited our arrival with T-bone steaks. Such a deal. Everybody loved this guy.

4

England: Next Stop Normandy

THE 50TH FIGHTER GROUP'S three squadrons each had its own airstrip on the Channel coast near Southampton. Since the Ninth Air Force engineers didn't have time to sit around and watch concrete dry they quickly constructed runways of pre-fab steel matting. These proved adequate for fighter planes and some bombers. We were all surprised and somewhat disappointed to discover that we were the owners of twenty-four brand new Republic Aviation P-47 Thunderbolts (replacing the P-51s). First impressions of the massive P-47 both amazed and appalled some of the pilots. The P-47 weighed 10,000 pounds empty and 19,000 pounds fully loaded with eight .50 caliber machine guns and 2,500 pounds of bombs and rockets. By comparison, a British Spitfire weighed 5,600 pounds empty and 7,500 pounds loaded. A lot of the young pilots wondered if they could safely fly the huge fighter, let alone fight with it.

But their fears were soon quieted when they began flying combat missions from England into France across the Channel. The big fighter's speed, strength and hitting power quickly made it one of the war's deadliest weapons. It could take massive amounts of damage and still get its pilot safely home. Until the P-47s arrived, liquid-cooled inline engines powered most front line fighters (like the P-51). The Thunderbolts were powered by 2,000 horsepower radial engines, combined with four-bladed propellers. P-51s were more maneuverable but more easily brought down when enemy fire pierced the metal tubes carrying its liquid coolant.

In the entire history of military aviation many say there has never been an airplane that could match the Republic P-47 for ruggedness and dependability. It had a speed of 428 miles an hour and a range 925 miles. It was the most effective killing machine in World War II.

The 10th flew its first combat mission, a fighter sweep near Caen, France the first week in May. The 47s attacked marshalling yards, railroad bridges and factories. During the rest of the month we lost two aircraft. In one, the pilot was badly injured and had to bail out over the Channel. He was rescued the same day. The other plane crashed on takeoff at Lymington and burst into a huge ball of orange flame. The pilot walked away from it. How he got that lucky I don't know.

I began doing photography and left the bombs and machine guns to my pals in armament. I did all the gun camera work, which meant I loaded the planes with motion picture film before a mission and made sure the cameras were working. Then when the planes returned I unloaded the film and got it processed. A pretty neat deal. Between this and KP and guard duty it took almost twenty-four hours a day. I made time in the late evenings to write home. We didn't have any lights but really didn't miss them because you could sit outside and watch the sun set about 11 P.M. It got dark about midnight and dawn appeared at two in the morning. Weird.

About this time I was on a convoy detail, a two-day journey across England. Twenty of us went to a quartermaster depot and drove back twenty new jeeps. You can see a lot of that country in a couple of days. The first night out we slept across the road from the ruins of a Norman castle. There wasn't much left but you could still see what remained of the old moat—and it had water in it. Inside the ruins were old dungeons and passageways, just like the movies. It was a strange feeling to be sitting in a modern jeep and trying to visualize that on the very same spot knights in armor were fighting wars a thousand years ago (poor bastards). We passed other castles, one of them unbelievably large, right out of Robin Hood. Britain was crawling with history. The green countryside lived up to its reputation.

My fondest memory of our brief stay in England, however, was on a two-day pass and a train ticket to London. Freedom at last. The streets were a sea of khaki; thousands of American soldiers all looking for a good time. I had arranged to meet with my uncle, Charles Little, who had an office there at Supreme Allied Headquarters. Charles was a captain in the Signal Corps and had recently arrived in London from a long tour of duty in North Africa. He didn't like his new desk assignment and was trying to get into a combat unit (he finally did and saw action in France and Germany). This great man, with turquoise blue eyes, had always been like a father to me. He was Gary Cooper, John Wayne and Clint Eastwood rolled into one. We met in Piccadilly Circus —just walked up and shook hands and looked at each other. Then we had a huge roast beef dinner on the main drag, talked for hours and finally said our farewells. I spent the next two hours in the blackest of London blackouts looking for the American Red Cross and a place to sleep. I'd never seen so many Americans in my life.

The German robot bombs were the next things to get my attention in Lymington. They were more like a highflying torpedo than a bomb. This slow moving rocket was the V-1, and it was timed to go off indiscriminately any place in England. You could hear the thing coming because of its slow speed and it was always a little scary when its rocket motor stopped. You knew it was up there and about to drop on you. It scared hell out of the civilian population because no one on the ground could know when it was timed to cut out and drop. Most people simply called it the buzz bomb or robot bomb, but some of our guys called it the rowboat bomb. I asked one GI why he called it that. "Well," he said, "Because it sounds just like a rowboat." I guessed he meant motorboat, because the thing did sound sort of like a motorboat.

By the middle of May in 1944 England was literally overrun with American soldiers, hundreds of thousands of them—and hundreds of airfields. Some people thought of us as guests of the British, and considering our overwhelming numbers the British and the Americans got along pretty well. Most Americans behaved like guests and most of the British liked the Yanks in spite of their American brashness. The bottom line was that the British knew we were there to provide the help they so desperately needed.

I never did get another pass to London but neither did most of the GIs. The reason: there had been an amazing build-up of men and materiel along the southern Channel coast for months. Now our little airstrip was landlocked, and MPs were everywhere on the perimeters to keep the hundreds of units contained inside this loop. There were gigantic trucks and bulldozers, armored cars, Sherman tanks, field kitchens, heavy artillery; everything needed to wage war—including the personnel.

You didn't have to be a German spy to know an invasion was imminent. The big question was only where and when it would take place. Near the English Channel coast every country road and village was parked solid with men and machines hidden under the trees and bushes, just waiting to go.

5

Normandy: Operation Overlord

By the first of June 1944 the buildup of men and machines had created unbelievable activity in southern England. Along with our Allies, an army of three and a half million men gathered in Britain with the planes, ships, tanks, ammunition, fuel, rations, clothing, medicines and you name it needed to sustain this coming invasion. Britain was top-heavy with troops, and General Eisenhower jokingly said, "Only the great number of barrage balloons floating constantly in British skies kept the islands from sinking under the seas."

All the troops were sealed in their camps behind barbed wire and armed guards, and we were not even allowed to write letters to our families. Since our squadron was pretty well cut off from civilization we saw very few civilians and actually missed hearing the little kids shouting, "Got any gum, Yank?" GIs everywhere were busy waterproofing their vehicles and I was assigned a new jeep and a driver named Junior. He was a nice kid from Oklahoma, just out of high school and a hell of a good truck driver.

The deal was, everybody was responsible for making his vehicle waterproof. The management assured us that if the jeep drowned out and we got blown away in three feet of water, don't come cryin' back to them for sympathy. This got my attention right away. The idea was to cover all the electrical connectors, the ignition and generator and other sensitive parts. Since I didn't know where to locate these, Junior was quite happy to art direct me. We covered all these brand new parts with a dark gray gunk that resembled cup grease and it stuck like chewing gum. So that water wouldn't get sucked into the exhaust pipe, we attached a flexible hose to the end of it and ran it straight up in the air. Brilliant. The ordinance guys rigged me a .50-caliber machine gun on a metal post anchored between the front and back seats. It would move almost all the way around and still not be aimed at Junior's head. A heavy box of ammunition lay in the back with me.

Looking back through the years, lots of things get fuzzy. I do remember writing my mother and asking her to send me several paint brushes (which she did), but I have no idea of the approximate date. At any rate the timing was perfect. One of the pilots said he heard I was a super artist and wanted to hire me to paint a large Daisy Mae on the cowling of his P-47. The truth was that the only art I ever got paid for was in my senior year at Austin High School when I worked after school painting posters with good friends Wally Sheid and Joe Parrish. I think we charged twenty cents each. Later I painted gaudy back-bar murals for the Grand Prize Brewery. My first effort was painting a Mexican with a big sombrero and sandals leaning against a saguaro cactus. Hardly original but they loved it. Soon all the South El Paso bar owners wanted one. I hadn't seen a good picture of Daisy Mae since I last read the *El Paso Times* funnies. And I knew little Daisy was going to be tough. I thought about asking the pilot if he wouldn't prefer a painting on his plane of a Mexican leaning on a cactus. I hastened to tell him I was no Michelangelo but I'd

*Fine art soared to new heights in the European Theater of Operations.
A fighter pilot paid me a one-pound note for my rendering of Daisy Mae
on his P-47. Those are Invasion Stripes on the wing.*

like to do it. I asked him if he also wanted me to letter Daisy May
in big letters that would stretch all the way from the cowling to
the cockpit. He said, " Just paint Gallopin' Gertie." I guess his
girlfriend's name was Gertie. Anyway, he loved the finished job
and paid me a one-pound note, which was about four dollars.

Operation Overlord was the code name for the Allied invasion
of German occupied France. Code names of the American beaches
were Utah and Omaha, separated by several miles. Juno, Gold
and Sword were the British and Canadian names for their landing sites in Normandy. It is so well documented that I can't add
much to D-Day, June 6, 1944, except that from where I sat I
should tell you it is one of the most amazing military stories of all
time. The invasion was originally planned for June 5 but on the
night of June 4 the weather was so bad and the Channel was so
rough, Eisenhower took a huge gamble and postponed every-

thing until June 6. It turned out to be a good gamble. Good enough for 150,000 men to wade ashore that day. But a lot of them didn't make it to the beach sand. Some tank crews skewed off the landing ramps of their LSTs (Landing Ship, Tank) and drowned in fifteen feet of water. The 10th Squadron's planes flew the first fighter-bomber sweeps over the beaches, taking off at 2:45 in the morning of the 6th. Our planes were flying constantly, some getting hit but returning several times a day from missions. Most of the pilots flew three missions that day. All Allied planes were identified by broad striping (about 12 inches wide) painted front to back on the wings and on all sides of the fuselage. The black and white stripes sent a clear message to Allied ground troops: "Don't shoot at me."

The mission of the 10th was providing close air support for U.S. and Allied ground troops, flying dive-bombing missions against troop concentrations, enemy airfields, bridges, railroads— anything that could be destroyed at low level. Lots of time these P-47s would return from missions with tree limbs and telephone wires hanging on their wings.

The obvious way to accomplish ground support was to build fighter strips as close to the front lines as possible. And until the Ninth Air Force engineers could build these little strips we would operate from England. Some of the twenty-six advance landing fields in Normandy were built under direct German fire. American artillery units with armored half-tracks, anti-aircraft guns and anti-tank guns protected the engineers and their heavy equipment. Even a week after D-Day the Allies had only tentative strips of beachhead along the Normandy coast. I doubt if most Americans back home had the foggiest idea of what a small piece of beach property their army controlled.

About ten days after D-Day we got the word that several airstrips were ready for Ninth Air Force squadrons to come ashore. We'd been living in tents and griping our heads off about the

Ninth Air Force shoulder patch.

incessant rain finding its way inside. But now that we were alerted for a trip to the beach, we had to give up our tents, leaving us only two wet wool blankets and a little collection of straw to sleep on (even after all these years I still keep bitching).

Next stop, Southampton—just a few miles from our Lymington airfield. And since we'd had a ringside seat overlooking the Channel on D-Day I think all of us were impatient to really do something, not just sit there. We knew this would go down in history as a very big deal. When we left the marshaling area they gave each of us a carton of cigarettes, six boxes of K rations, canned heat (to do our own cooking), chewing gum, invasion money, flea powder, and seasick pills. The K rations were almost a treat after eating C rations the whole time in England. The Ks were not too bad—if you didn't have to eat them as a steady diet. We had three kinds—breakfast, dinner and supper. They were all in khaki-colored waxed boxes about the size of a box of Cracker-jacks. As I remember, the dinner menu included a can of Kraft cheese, several dog biscuits, a package of lemon powder (to make juice), a lump of sugar, four cigarettes, a box of dextrose tablets and a piece of chewing gum. The supper ration consisted of a little can of Spam, biscuits, bouillon powder, coffee powder, sugar, a bitter, non-melt chocolate bar, four cigarettes and gum. This stuff was highly concentrated, and if you ate it too fast you were sure to get sick. It was surprising how these little Ks would fill you up. I don't remember what the breakfast box consisted of but you can guess. Each box also contained several sheets of khaki-colored toilet paper. Jolly good.

In Southampton we were all sitting around the docks smoking and shooting the bull, watching hundreds of ships come and go, and this LST appears right in front of us. We really are going for a boat ride. As soon as this ominous-looking craft lands, two big doors in the front of the ship open wide and a steel ramp drops down on the wooden dock right where we are sitting. Next thing I saw were German soldiers, several hundred of them being herded out of the double doors. They were POWs (prisoners of war)—some of the first Germans to surrender in Normandy. They were dirty and muddy and bandaged, obviously wondering what was going to happen next. As they passed by us they looked our way with tired, unseeing eyes, perhaps thinking "the war is over for us but just beginning for you." I wondered what in the hell I was getting myself into. Looking back, I think we were lucky to see these bedraggled troops instead of the image we had of big goose-stepping supermen who might just chew us up for lunch. We were pretty fired up as we climbed the ramp with all our gear, trucks, jeeps and everything needed to launch a new airfield. Seemed like it was late afternoon and the Channel crossing was uneventful. We watched history's largest armada of ships going and coming as we headed for Omaha, about a hundred miles away. The 50th Group was to be one of the first three fighter outfits to make the move from England to France. Within three weeks of D-Day thirty-one Allied fighter squadrons were operating from the beachhead airstrips.

Another kid and I came ashore in a jeep at Omaha Beach in Normandy. The ships at right are LSTs (Landing Ship Tank). The Allies tied barrage balloons to steel cables to discourage enemy dive-bombers from coming down among us.

We mostly sat around all night wondering what tomorrow would bring. My associates (we were corporals by now—it had only taken a year and a half to get this far) dozed fitfully waiting for old Mangan to get seasick and start throwing up. They were taking bets. But I fooled them this time and kept swallowing seasick pills, feeling wonderful the whole trip watching hundreds of other ships around us. Finally, we saw the French coastline and in another few minutes the LST ground to a shuddering stop on the gently sloping beach. In the meantime, everybody piled into their trucks and weapons carriers, with Junior and me in our jeep. Junior hunched over the steering wheel and kept pleading with me not to fire the stupid machine gun. I kept trying to tell him they assured me that the gun wouldn't revolve far enough to hit his head. His comment: "Bullshit."

We hit the beach running in only about a foot and a half of seawater. It was shallow enough that we didn't really need all our waterproofing, but what the hell. There was an MP—I think they were called "beachmasters" about fifty yards up on the sand waving his arms and pointing to our left and shouting, "Move it off this goddamn beach!" Moving thousands of troops and all the weaponry was a massive undertaking, so that if even one unit didn't move out quickly men and machines would back up into the water and create the mother of all traffic jams. The fabled Luftwaffe only put up token raids on the beaches but German fighters were always a threat after D-Day, especially if troops and supplies were bunched up. America had dozens of barrage balloons in the air over the beaches, tethered to the ground with steel cables. The cables were easily capable of cutting German fighters in half. I saw lots of these balloons at Omaha Beach, but I never heard whether or not they brought down any German planes.

In all the confusion, our squadron became separated, so a small group (about twenty of us) stuck together and headed away from the mass of men and machines. We found a relatively low spot in the dunes and shrubs and pulled over into some Frenchman's apple orchard. All Quiet on the Western Front. We piled out and gathered around the lieutenant for guidance since he was the only officer in our intrepid bunch of killers. He knew as well as I did that we were lost and wanted to get as far away from the damn beach as possible. The main reason: German artillery was dug in several miles inland from the beaches, firing at no particular target, just hoping to hit large groups of men and mountains of supplies piled up on shore. The lieutenant knew the name of the town that was our destination, though, and he had a map. At that point I was extremely happy that I was a corporal and he was the lieutenant. Our destination was the town of Carentan, about six or eight miles from the Channel Coast. It was part of that narrow strip holding the beaches together, and it was under artillery fire day and night. Everybody was trying to get away from the beaches as well as from Carentan, our soon-to-be summer camp. What was funny about Carentan was that my favorite newspaper, *The Stars and Stripes*, had already set up shop there and was printing papers right in the middle of this mess.

The traffic was murder. I remember at one crossroads an MP stood right in the middle of the intersection pointing vehicles in different directions. I gained a lot of respect for these guys who stood a good chance of being flattened by a friendly tank or hit by a sniper's bullet from a church steeple a mile away. Gutsy guys.

And soon there it was in its Norman splendor, the new home of the 10th Squadron, called Landing Strip A-10 Carentan. Most of the other GIs had already dug in and the planes had landed safely on the steel mat runway. We were off and running.

My pal Junior screeched to a stop in the middle of our green pasture advance landing field just long enough to unload my gear and me. Then he slithered away in that jeep heading for what would soon become the squadron motor pool. I could hear his grateful sigh of relief when he got rid of Corporal Mangan and his scary machine gun. He roared off singing "Way down yonder in the Indian Nation...." At that juncture I became enamored quickly with another of man's noble inventions—the foxhole. I figured that each mile away from that beach would bring some semblance of peace and quiet. But no. It got noisier all the time. Our big guns were now behind us, and you could hear them go off as the shells came crackling over our heads aiming for the German lines. And the German artillery was mostly firing over our heads at American troops. At the risk of sounding repetitious I wondered again, "What the hell was I getting into here?" Eventually, though, it began to quiet down. Maybe the Germans ran out of shells—or people. I didn't want to dwell on that.

6

The Battle of the Hedgerows

"STINKING HEDGEROWS." That's the comment you'll get from anybody who spent the summer of 1944 in the province of Normandy. That part of France was divided into small plots of farmland bordered by hedgerows. The earthen walls were six to ten feet high and about five feet thick, woven solid with trees, thorn bushes and brush roots. Each one was a natural fortification, impenetrable even to tanks. Some plots would be about the size of a football field, others half that large. Each had narrow dirt roads, just wide enough for a farmer's horse cart to travel around the inside of the plot. My guess was that these hedgerows were centuries old, intended to mark properties and shield crops from violent sea winds. In 1944 the hedgerows played a huge part in mechanized warfare. You can understand how an invader might bog down permanently inside these barriers.

My armament buddies (who got there first) greeted my arrival in the hedgerows with their own stories of how to get lost in Normandy. Then they reveled in showing me their foxholes and telling me how dangerous it was around here. Ha, ha. They sat there smoking Luckies and watched me dig my foxhole. Actually, the digging was fairly easy since the ground was soft dark brown dirt, the exact opposite of El Paso's rocky caliche. My GI shovel (correct nomenclature: Tool, Entrenching, M1) was an engineering work of art. You could tilt the metal head at various degrees and use it for anything from a hatchet to a regular shovel. Such a deal.

How big is a foxhole? Keep it small, they said. About six feet long and three feet wide. This allows you enough room to lie down and gives you enough space for your personal junk. It also makes you almost invisible and fairly safe from enemy aircraft and artillery. Like most of the others, I spread my canvas shelter-half across the top edges, weighted with rocks to keep the rain out. Fat chance. June must have been the start of their rainy season because the rains drenched us day and night. Everything and everybody was soaked. This went on for a week, and then we had two beautiful sunny days in which we all got wonderfully dry—blankets and all. I even put a length of steel landing strip as a roof over my new home away from home. Next day the heavens opened up again and within minutes standing water was everywhere. The top and sides of my foxhole caved in, mud and all—right on those dry blankets. Mud was ankle deep. It was sort of pitiful, but as people kept saying, "Hey, there's a war on." *C'est la guerre* was absolutely the most used foreign phrase in this whole unpleasantness. For both sides the weather had to be responsible for much of the aggravation from 1939 to 1945. The experts said that 1944 set the record for being the stormiest, coldest and wettest in fifty years.

After the big cloudburst I spent part of the next day digging a new foxhole. The weather was still punk, low overcast, so the planes didn't fly any missions. I took the day off to line my foxhole with silk, and I had plenty of free material. On the way to

Carentan from the beach hundreds of American parachutes lay spread over the ground and dangled from the trees. Lots of GIs were wearing scarves made of green camouflaged silk left hurriedly by the 82nd and 101st Airborne Divisions as they cut most of the main roads leading from the mainland to the beaches. All through that lush Norman countryside lay wrecked gliders that cracked up trying to land at night, surrounded by hedgerows. Hundreds of GIs dropped into deep marshes flooded by the Germans and drowned burdened by hundred-pound packs, rifles and ammunition. These marshes hadn't been cleared and the ripe sweet stink of death and decay was awful. I couldn't get it out of my nose. From the looks of the crashed gliders those troops had a miserable chance of survival. The gliders were towed across the Channel by DC-3s, and cut loose to crash land in the dark. The Germans made it even worse by planting thousands of tall, heavy poles in the fields about ten feet apart so that many American gliders (made of canvas and wood) would break up on landing.

Back at the airstrip the weather turned bright and sunny, perfect for our fighter-bombers to do what we were being paid the big bucks to do. The pilots were flying two or three missions a day—and they didn't seem to mind. Those missions were short, some less than an hour, since the planes took off to strafe and bomb nearby German tanks, troops and anything that resembled a target. Lots of times you could see the P-47s receiving anti-aircraft fire before they reached full altitude

About this time the home office decided it should give me some help in winning the war, and they assigned Phil Pearce, a corporal from Kentucky, to do the job. Phil was an armorer but he also loved photography. Old lucky Frank. Eventually, we took on another armorer, a genius Italian kid from Brooklyn named Frank Comito who invented a way to develop motion picture film in a leaky tent. The only catch to this super deal was that we still had to load machine guns and bombs when the war became real busy. But it was okay with us. You didn't actually kill some-body face to face. You merely helped from a distance. Anyway, that's my story and I'm sticking to it.

Out on the flight line Pearce and I dug several foxholes, just in case. Sure enough, one morning coming right out of the sun was this Luftwaffe ME-109 heading right for us, machine guns popping away. You could see the black swastika on his tail. The tracers bounced around and we both dived into our new foxhole. I learned one thing on this little exercise, and that is if you get far enough below the surface they can't hit you. I haven't had this theory confirmed by military historians but I think it's right. This lone aircraft made one more pass at the field, damaging no one but tearing some ugly holes in the skin of several P-47s. Phil and I peeked cautiously over the top as the German flew off dodging bullets from our own anti-aircraft artillery that was located on our field. We looked at each other and strangely enough, started laughing. It was nice to be alive and well.

Ever since the sixth grade I had always wanted to know more about trench warfare in 1918, and doughboys and France and French civilians and mademoiselle from gay Paree parley voo. Stuff like that. So here I was in Normandy and there were lots of French villages and French people and I wanted to check them out. So I talked a buddy of mine into taking a look at Carentan with me. We were supposed to be restricted to our bivouac area, but who's counting every GI in Normandy? We both carried car-bines, as all of us were always armed, even to visit the bathroom (read outdoor latrine). Well that's the way it was. We passed the remains of several little towns that had been practically obliter-ated by both American and German artillery and bombs.

The French were generally friendly to Americans, but some had mixed feelings and you couldn't blame them. In order to cut German supply lines, American and British bombers literally leveled lots of towns. The French were freed of their hated

German masters at the cost of total destruction (in many cases). There were lots of little kids running alongside us, waving and asking for candy and gum. Our supplies didn't last long but even so, you never saw a kid who didn't love you. They had seen *beaucoup* Americans by this time, late June 1944, and most of them were wearing American overseas caps, short pants, knee-high wool stockings and wooden shoes (as in pictures of little Dutch boys). Some of the kids really looked kind of sad— about ten years old, wearing a pair of size eleven GI shoes. Girls and women also wore wooden shoes. The men, most of them farmers, wore blue cotton pants and shirts, suspenders and old woolen suit jackets. Some even wore ties. It took me a while to get used to seeing these farmers wearing ancient sport coats and walking behind plows pulled by big heavy draft horses. Not a green John Deere in sight. Headgear was always a wool cap with a little bill and men's footwear was invariably rubber boots. But they smiled broadly and saluted and seemed generally happy to see *les Americains*.

Another thing. I had always envisioned Frenchmen as being rather dark skinned, with black hair and little pencil-thin mustaches, probably wearing a tam and smoking a long cigarette. (Turns out the only thing I was right about was the smoking, and half of the smokers were ten-year-old boys.) Everywhere I looked in Carentan I saw blonds and redheads and fair skin. What's going on here? Seems this genetic soup goes all the way back to the 800s A.D. and the invasion of the Norsemen. These fierce, seafaring Vikings came from Norway and other parts of Scandinavia. They were predominately blond, blue eyed, seamen who eventually liked what they saw and approved of the French weather and pretty girls. So they stayed and created what we still see today, Normandy courtesy of the Norsemen.

There was a later invasion by Germanic tribes in 911 A.D. King Charles the Simple (really) mounted this incursion. He appointed a chieftain with the rather unromantic name of Rollo to head up what was then the duchy of Normandy. Rollo's most famous descendant had the more belligerent name of William the Conqueror. He won the Battle of Hastings in 1066, forever changing the look of England. In some ways I felt the look of France was more attractive than England's, perhaps because it was not so well manicured.

You don't need to thank me for these profound observations.

7

Just When You Thought It Was Safe...

WHO CAN FORGET the movie *Jaws*? As I recollect, it became an American motion picture icon during the 1970s and scared people half to death with its tight shots of this great white shark about to swallow a skinny-dipping girl in shallow water. Hollywood soon followed its success with a sequel named (what else) *Jaws II*. The producers came up with a single powerful promotion that screamed, "Just when you thought it was safe to go back in the water..." What happened was that after the safe climax in the original picture, the townspeople became complacent and returned to the beach in large numbers. Little did they know that gliding silently through four feet of water a few yards away was another great white getting ready to eat a ten-year-old kid. Panic time.

A similarity involved the 10th Fighter Squadron in early July 1944. The United States Army (we were officially in the Army Air Corps, since the separate Air Force did not yet exist) began bringing USO Shows to Normandy to inject a little fun into sagging troop morale. Especially if the troops could be brought back to a relatively safe place. The hedgerow campaign was sort of bogging down, and night skies were not always like the Fourth of July. So just when the brass thought it was safe to bring entertainers to our little sliver of Normandy, they brought us a USO Show. It didn't include Bob Hope and famous movie stars and a grateful audience of several thousand soldiers. But we got to see Spike Jones and his City Slickers along with two gorgeous blonds. The entire audience was no more than two hundred of us sitting on the ground with me on the front row holding a Box Brownie camera. Spike and his gang of idiots performed on a flat bed trailer and they were a solid hit with songs like *Vee Heil, Vee Heil Right in der Fuhrer's Face* accompanied with police whistles, cymbals and other weird instruments. And the two girls with their silver-spangled short skirts and ankle-strap high heels were dynamite. The GIs went nuts. They hadn't laid eyes on an American girl for months. Anyway, right in the middle of this entire racket, we heard a familiar sound screeching overhead, then a loud boom. For a moment it looked like der Fuhrer was about to ruin our show. The GIs sat dead still for a split second, then began looking around for a place to hide. But the funny thing was, both girls put their hands over their ears and shouted into the mike they were okay—and on with the show. Old Spike and his crew continued playing as though nothing unusual was happening. The shelling went on for another ten minutes, and then it got nice and quiet. The soldiers cheered and whistled and seemed real proud of these American civilians. I know I was.

Meanwhile, the war in the hedgerows groaned on. The Germans conveniently penned up our armored divisions in the fields of Normandy because even the big Sherman tanks couldn't navigate through the hedgerow barriers. They would try crashing through only to wind up stuck about half way. Then their front ends and lightly armored underbellies were openly exposed to

AMERICAN RED CROSS

Form 2047

— OF COURSE, A PERSON SHOULD NOT FOR FORM AN OPINION OF THE ENGLISH DRABNESS AT THIS POINT— BECAUSE THESE PEOPLE HAVE BEEN AT WAR FOR FIVE LONG YEARS — & TO MAKE MATTERS WORSE THEY'VE HAD IT *LITERALLY* DUMPED IN THEIR OWN BACK YARDS. — THEY HAVE BEEN BOMBED OUT PLENTY OF TIMES— & I CAN SAY FIRST HAND THAT THEY ARE STILL GETTING A LOT OF THAT. — THEY ARE REALLY STICKING IT OUT — & I'LL BET A LOT OF WOULD-BE AMERICANS WOULD HAVE CALLED IT QUITS LONG BEFORE NOW — HAD THEY BEEN IN THE SHOES OF THESE PEOPLE ∘

▓▓▓▓▓ BEFORE THE WAR WAS A ▓▓▓▓ TOWN, & I SUPPOSE BEFORE EVERYTHING BECAME RATIONED, IT WAS QUITE LIVELY. — IT IS VERY TYPICAL;— WITH A BEAUTIFUL PARK IN THE CENTER OF TOWN — WITH THE GREENEST GRASS YOU EVER SAW. — THEY SAY THE BEACH WAS SWELL BEFORE THE WAR — BUT NOW IT IS STRUNG WITH BARBED WIRE ENTANGLEMENTS —, & A PEACE-LOVING GUY IN SEARCH OF A SWIM WOULD SURELY GET SHOT — & NO QUESTIONS ASKED. ▓▓▓▓ IT'S HARD TO JUDGE THE SIZE OF AN ENGLISH CITY, BUT OFFHAND, I'D SAY ▓▓▓▓ IS ABOUT THE SIZE OF ▓▓▓▓ IT HAS SEVERAL NICE THEATRES; INCIDENTLY, ROY ROGERS IN "SONG OF TEXAS" WAS PLAYING AT ONE OF THEM.

— ENTERTAINMENT THESE DAYS IS HARD TO FIND —. THERE ARE PLENTY OF PUBS,— BUT THEY ARE PACKED & JAMMED EVERY NIGHT. THE AMERICAN RED CROSS HAS DONE WONDERFULLY — & I BELIEVE ANY AMERICAN SOLDIER WILL SAY THAT IT HAS SAVED THE DAY FOR THE YANK OVERSEAS. —

— BOY, I JUST HEARD A HOT PROGRAM ON THE RADIO! WISH YOU COULD HAVE HEARD IT AS I KNOW YOU WOULD HAVE BEEN INTERESTED.

Letters from overseas were always censored. This is the way a typical letter looked when the censor got through cutting out words with a razor blade. My handwriting was not all that good so I always printed my letters home. Still do. I sometimes wondered if our letters to America baffled the German secret agents.

41

direct hits from 88mm German artillery hidden in the next hedgerow. The tanks were taking a beating and the Allies were getting nowhere. An American sergeant named Culin conceived the idea of fabricating sort of a cowcatcher and welding it to the front of a tank. What to make it out of? There were tons of discarded steel underwater obstacles rusting on the nearby invasion beaches. They looked like giant "jacks" and had apparently not done too much damage to Allied equipment on D-day. So the armored divisions began turning some of them into razor-sharp v-shaped blades, then welding them to the front of tanks. Soon foundries back in England started fabricating huge steel forks on the vehicles. With this innovation Allied tanks could batter their way through a hedgerow with guns blazing. Good, but not good enough.

It seemed clear that the Allies badly needed to break out of this stalemate or we'd be stuck forever in Normandy. The schedule was way behind the planning timetable. More troops poured into Normandy, and they came ashore in the deep-water port of Cherbourg instead of landing on the beaches. Masses of heavy equipment flowed in and headed for Carentan, Saint-Mere-Eglise and other nearby villages close to the front lines. Saint-Mere was the town where an American paratrooper landed on top of a church, his parachute shrouds entangled in the steeple. He hung there all night trying to avoid being seen by German troops below. At times the narrow roads were bumper to bumper with the amazing output of American factories. One stalled truck, however, and you've got a major traffic jam. So about every half mile you would see stenciled signs nailed to roadside trees reading AREA UNDER ARTILLERY FIRE. MAINTAIN 60-YARD INTERVAL. There were also a great number of signs reading MINES CLEARED TO HEDGES. Others warned drivers to SLOW DOWN, DUST DRAWS FIRE.

When American heavy equipment like bulldozers, trucks,

In Normandy Corporal Kenny Wheeler steers us in the right direction. American road signs proved invaluable to GIs traveling along the unfamiliar country lanes all over Normandy. One stalled vehicle could create bumper-to-bumper traffic jams and invite German artillery.

graders and trailers rumbled through towns the French stared in amazement at the enormity of it all. Some trailers had tires considerably taller than a man's head. Even as an American I was impressed. When I saw all those tanks and guns and trucks I could understand why it took several years for America to get rolling, and I was glad I was on our side.

There were Yanks everywhere—few Frenchmen and not even any British where we were. Many of us pulled guard duty at night, but it wasn't all that bad. Two hours on and two hours off. When my two hours were up, I'd wake up the next guy, and so on. You were so pooped, you could fall back to sleep in seconds. We were told not to even think about lighting a cigarette at night. The squadron adjutant said that lighting a cigarette could easily be seen from a mile away, and who was I to argue? So I started chewing tobacco every night. A lot of the guys also started chewing, and dipping snuff. But cigarettes and other tobacco were free courtesy of Uncle Sam. Once a week on ration day you got in line and some sergeant handed you a carton of cigarettes. Such a deal.

One thing about pulling guard in Normandy, it was nearly always pitch dark and your body sort of melted into the hedgerows. The chances of somebody sneaking up behind you were zero to none. It gave me quality time to myself and I spent lots of hours contemplating my mortality and stuff like that. One time about midnight I was standing on the side of a little road guarding the entire Free World when I heard this low rumble from the direction of the beaches. Then I began to see tanks—bunched together and, naturally, running without lights. They were huge, almost black olive drab monsters with large white stars on the turrets. As each tank materialized out of the ground fog I could see that it had an open hatch with a faint glow coming out, lighting the face of a GI tanker. These faces all seemed to have a similar determined, no-nonsense look about them. There was an eerie light around their heads as they peered straight ahead and side to side. It was a startling, even sort of scary sight in the otherwise pitch darkness. Hollywood special effects could never have duplicated this shot.

I felt lucky to be alive and not a German who would soon have to face these guys head on. I have remembered this little scenario (if you could call it that) many times since. And I'm not sure why except that it imprinted a stark black and white impression on my brain.

By this time it was mid July. The weather improved, and the squadron flew more missions than ever, mainly dive bombing and strafing German airfields to keep the Luftwaffe from doing the same to us. But German fighters were still a force to be reckoned with. Phil Pearce and I went down to the flight line with a load of gun camera film one sunny morning. The flight line wasn't really a straight line of planes; they were staggered, with some hidden under trees and large hedges so an enemy fighter couldn't make a straight run and destroy them. Suddenly we heard this familiar pop pop pop as two ME 109s came out of nowhere, and as usual seemed (to us anyway) to be seeking out Pearce and me. Our friendly two-man foxhole was not close enough but there was a thick stone wall right near the flight line. We jumped behind the wall as the planes came zooming in, missing us a mile. Just as we were congratulating ourselves for our quick thinking, the planes made a lazy U-turn and headed back. Lead was ricocheting and dirt was flying in every direction. We jumped back to the other side of the wall, with equally safe results, and as the Germans flew off we shook hands again.

8

Friendly Fire: The Saint-Lo Breakout

It was seven weeks after D-Day. I pulled guard duty one night and was catching up on some sleep. My foxhole-underground home was still damp and uncomfortable from previous incessant rains. So I was lying on a blanket on top of the ground, covered by another blanket, with my feet facing the foxhole. Next to that was a deluxe hole fashioned by my good friend, Sandy Schwarz, a sergeant from New York. He used runway matting and tarpaper for a roof and it was impressive—large and rather elegant. We were about twenty feet apart, dug in beneath the branches of this huge old oak tree for protection from the elements.

I hadn't thought much about it, but since D-Day the Allies had moved practically nowhere in Normandy because of tremendous opposition from the German army. I'm pretty sure you're tired of hearing about hedgerows but it turned out they were most of the problem—each was a natural fortification. The 10th Fighter Squadron was still taking artillery fire almost every night, but in spite of it, some of us got so tired of living underground we decided to put up tents. Living on top of the ground had its advantages; not so wet and muddy and cramped. But the down side was, you'd no sooner get to sleep than the artillery came shrieking in. Then you'd pile out of the blankets half asleep and jump back into foxholes. It seemed to me that it was almost like a game for the Germans. They weren't hitting much, but psychologically they were rapidly driving us nuts, and they knew it. I thought seriously about staying with the tent and getting a decent night's sleep. I've never been one for quick decisions, so eventually I decided to play it safe and depend on the foxhole. The Allied advance from the beaches slowed and then all but stopped. Each foot gained was paid for by a heavy loss in men and equipment. I found out later that by this time some 20,000 Allied troops had died and another 20,000 were wounded. The Germans weren't taking prisoners since they didn't have facilities to hold them. But in some cases, neither did we. To put it mildly, the war had its nasty downside.

Then the Allies mounted a huge air-ground effort, code named Operation Cobra, designed to open a gap in German lines that Allied infantry and armored divisions could plunge through. Cobra would begin with a massive, pulverizing air bombardment and artillery shelling of the German defenses. Allied planners selected an area outside the town of Saint-Lo for the breakthrough attempt, a target roughly five miles long and two miles wide. It was to be saturated with bombs from the American Eighth and Ninth Air Forces and heavies from the Royal Air Force. Cobra began on July 24 but rain postponed most of the operation after American planes mistakenly bombed our own troops. Next day the fighter-bombers came in first, followed by Eighth Air Force B-17s and B-24s and RAF Lancasters, Wellingtons, and Halifaxes. They all flew in columns to a point directly over our little airstrip at Carentan. Every three minutes a bomber or fighter group checked in with our controller and then flew straight to Saint-Lo, which was about six or seven miles away. More than 3,000 planes "carpet bombed" the outskirts of Saint-Lo and I'm convinced that term was invented on the 24th and 25th of July 1944.

American ground troops had been pulled back from near Saint-Lo to allow for a margin of error on the part of the bombers. Opposing forces were separated by as little as 1,000 yards. But unfortunately, nature again took a hand in this mission. Destruction on the ground from the first waves of planes created huge black dust clouds, and a brisk wind blew them back over American troops. The next wave of bombers mistook these clouds to be target markers and began bombing our own troops. The luckless 30th Infantry Division suffered 814 casualties including 64 killed. A bomber dropped its load on one of our sister airstrips, the 404th Fighter Group, at a nearby hamlet called Chipelle. This mistake killed four men, wounded fourteen, and destroyed two P-47s on the ground. Also killed that day by friendly fire was American three-star General Leslie McNair who was monitoring the attack from a foxhole in the front line.

Speaking of friendly fire, where was old Frank at the start of what became the greatest air raid in history? In the sack, of course, just trying to catch a few well-deserved winks after protecting part of the Ninth Air Force all night. So I'm snoozing there under our leafy oak tree minding my own business when suddenly I hear the loudest, most frightening sound imaginable. I knew in seconds it had to be a bomb since a tremendous concussion hit me, and the ground shook like an earthquake. First, I tried to open my eyes to see what happened, but I couldn't see anything. Nada. And I thought, *oh shit!* Then I realized it was just dirt covering my eyes so I started to move my hands and arms to get rid of the damn dirt. But nothing moved. Now I was really scared; I hate that. Somebody drops a bomb on you and you can't move your limbs? Hail Mary Full of Grace...

Next I heard lots of shouting and the friendly voice of Sandy Schwarz. "Jesus, F. J. (he always called me F. J.) are you okay?" I didn't know exactly how to answer, but I said, "Get me out of here and maybe I can tell you!" Sandy and a bunch of the other guys grabbed shovels. They scraped and clawed the fresh earth, pulled me away from the bomb crater and I quickly moved my arms and legs. Everything worked perfectly, I'm extremely happy to tell you. But I was completely disoriented, primarily because our big oak tree was gone. It had just vanished in a split second, and everything else looked strange and different. Schwarz' foxhole was gone, as was mine—and others. Everything had that otherworld look. It was kind of dreamlike. I sat back down on the GI blanket and it felt like something was searing my butt. So I looked underneath and there was the culprit; something I'd never seen before, a large shard of steel from an exploding bomb. This piece of shrapnel was about ten inches long and it was white hot. Then I looked around and there were lots of other pieces, all jagged, razor sharp, hot as hell, and scary looking. They burned holes right through the blanket as well as most of my other junk. I was sitting there with one shoe on, wearing a torn pair of khaki shorts. The medics arrived in minutes and pronounced me fit. But we're talking stress here.

I began taking inventory of my gear and there wasn't much left. Gone was a new Zippo lighter my mother had sent me, my harmonica, my fountain pen, and all my other personal stuff. I will always wonder what happens to things like this, as well as to unexploded shells and grenades, rifles, canteens, even uniforms and helmets. Most shells don't really hit anything; millions of them just zing by and disappear into thin air. I suppose this stuff gets plowed under by French farmers trying to replant their apple orchards. Very likely it will keep turning up for centuries, and a thousand years from now some Frenchman will say, "What in the HELL is this?

Mangan (top right) after friendly fire. This is the shell hole created by a wayward bomb that missed me by two inches. I was left with one shoe, torn khaki shorts, and a shredded carbine.

My carbine didn't disappear, but it might as well have. The barrel was bent and the wooden stock shredded. Strangely enough, my web belt and canteen survived the holocaust. I still have that canteen and I looked at it the other day. Plainly stamped on the metal bottom are the letters U.S. Army 1918. I guess they hadn't heard of planned obsolescence in the War to End all Wars. Or maybe it was just a good design, since today's GIs still carry the identical canteens hanging on the identical web belts. I also looked at my old helmet while writing this piece. It still has a

Sandy Schwarz (in tee shirt) digging for his personal stuff after the bombing.

rectangular white stripe about an inch deep and maybe three inches wide stenciled on the back, right on the bottom. They never told us the reason for it but the rumor was that if the stripe suddenly turned yellow, don't ask, just put on your mask because you're getting hit with mustard gas.

Meanwhile, back to the errant bomb, everybody was standing around looking at a sky full of heavy bombers and asking me how come I didn't get killed. Our ordinance experts surmised that it was a combination of two things: the ground was super saturated with water from weeks of constant rain, causing the bomb (five hundred pounds) to penetrate before blowing up underground. This caused the main force of the blast to go upward rather than outward (leaving me sort of under the blast). The crater was fifty feet wide and twenty-five feet deep. My feet were on the very edge of that hole, a fact that caused me and all the rest of the experts to conclude that if my feet had been even two or three inches closer to the edge the blast would have taken my feet off at the ankles. I thought, Jesus Christ, I'd rather be dead. After Saint-Lo I did a lot of introspection, something I'd never done much of before. The concussion caused some ear ringing but that went away shortly. I'm just lucky I guess.

The troops stood there looking up in the sky at all those bombers. Actually, and I'm not stretching it here, the sky was literally black with planes—wing tip to wing tip. Thousands and thousands of them blotted out the sun. As far as I know there has never been a sight like this before or since. The sound of bombs hitting the ground was ear splitting and terrifying; they hit so fast it sounded like a gigantic machine gun, like all the noises in the world rolled into one. This had to be hell on the German troops since every shell hole touched every other one. There was no place to hide from this saturation. The bombers kept coming in formation kind of like a conveyor belt, checking in with the ground controller at our A-10 strip at Carentan and making their left turn right over our heads. But they also took their share of punishment. I watched open mouthed as B-17s were hit by German anti-aircraft and spun helplessly to the ground. Crews in some of the heavies bailed out and I counted the chutes as they blossomed open, knowing that there were ten men in each crew. Sometimes all ten would get out, but usually only about five made it, and you had no idea if they were badly wounded and would live through it. I really felt sorry for these guys, especially when a bomber got hit and burst into a ball of flame. There was no way out. It was a hell of a way to die. And to think that I once wanted to fly and take aerial pictures from one of these bombers.

For the German troops on the ground it was like the end of the world. A German panzer commander later said he watched in disbelief as the monster armada appeared. "The planes kept coming over and the bomb carpets unrolled in great rectangles. My anti-aircraft hardly opened its mouth when the batteries received direct hits, which knocked out half the guns and silenced the rest. After an hour I had no communication with anybody, even by radio. By noon nothing was visible but dust and smoke."

So many of his troops lost their lives in this carpet bombing and so many others were wounded or numb with shock, or babbling incoherently that for all practical purposes his panzer division no longer existed. One Ninth Air Force P-38 group carried two belly tanks of Napalm on each of its planes, adding more flaming horror to the target. No question about it, the breakout at Saint-Lo in Normandy would go down in the history books as one of the mightiest battles of World War II. It was as important as D-Day, the fall of Paris, or the crossing of the Rhine.

Then the bombing slowed and finally stopped. The next thing we saw was a squad of 30th Division riflemen bursting into our bivouac area, badly shaken and mad as hell at me of all people. With only my khaki shorts on I guess I looked like I'd just spent the day getting a Coppertone tan while they were getting bombed. Their sergeant was about ready to kill. He looked me in the eye and demanded, "You sons of bitches trying to kill us?" I said, "No, we're trying to kill ME!" Then he saw my yawning bomb crater and everybody's stuff scattered all over the ground and he simmered down. The U.S. Army slowly turned around and started slogging back toward Saint-Lo.

Minutes before the bomb dropped, my buddy Sandy Schwarz (who would later become a prominent Madison Avenue publisher) was coming back to his foxhole after noon chow. He had a habit of getting in a few winks when possible and was heading for his abode when he noticed that a shipment of cigarettes had arrived. He waited in line about five minutes and picked up his ration of a carton of Camels. Sandy was a heavy smoker in those days and was taking his time getting back when the bomb exploded. He said later, "Just imagine it in print, Saved by a Carton of Camels! What an ad that would make."

After Saint-Lo the hedgerow war was almost over. Allied infantry and armored divisions poured through huge breaks in the undefended hedges as the Germans retreated under withering fire. Our armored divisions finally clanked out of Normandy's sodden, murderous fields and moved onto firm, dry rolling plains, made to order for tank warfare. Enter General George Patton and his Third Army. He didn't play an active part in the D-Day Invasion as most people thought, but after Saint-Lo his Third Army began moving rapidly across France. Patton was not well liked by the GIs and it was our destiny in the 10th to become part of the Third Army. He demanded clean, well-dressed soldiers —not an army that looked like us. But after living underground for the past few months most Americans didn't look much like recruiting posters. So one of his first official orders was a notice that from now on all E.M. (enlisted men) would be properly attired. Officers were already properly attired. Patton liked the word "personnel" and he used that a lot. Personnel in the field under his command would wear helmets at all times. Personnel would carry carbines, rifles, sidearms or sub-machine guns, and get this: personnel would also wear ties. I couldn't believe this. Imagine taking your chances of getting killed wearing a tie. Jesus.

The tie thing never caught on but it provided us with some laughs. Actually, old Patton was about half right. Most of the soldiers under his new command were a pretty raggedy-ass bunch. We wore everything from stocking caps to baseball caps. To replace what I lost during the recent bomb blast our supply sergeant issued me some natty retread clothing—nice and clean. A number of the 10th Fighter Squadron GIs found some motherly French women to wash their clothes for a pack of cigarettes. The Germans continued retreating after their defeat at Saint-Lo and we started living above ground in tents. It was wonderful. The weather was pretty good and, weather permitting, the pilots kept flying two or three missions a day. The first week in August they had a field day. George Kiser, who was now a lieutenant colonel in 50th Group Headquarters, led a flight of four P-47s on a mission to bomb several highway bridges to slow the retreating Germans. The weather turned sour and nobody could see the ground because of low cloud cover. The Thunderbolts were in the act of aborting the mission when the colonel radioed the three other P-47s that he was going down to take one more look—maybe see the ground anyway. He went down through the heavy cloudbank, and the countryside appeared clearly as if by magic, along with a two-lane road, bumper to bumper with retreating German trucks, tanks, halftracks and horse-drawn artillery.

Kiser radioed his pilots and they hit the convoy within seconds taking turns strafing and bombing the column. They radioed back to group headquarters calling for more planes, and once they arrived the carnage became unbelievable. What the pilots would do to retreating columns was to roar down maybe twenty feet above the ground and take out the lead two or three vehicles. These would usually burst into flame, leaving the rest of the convoy stalled with no place to run or hide, since many of those French country roads had only two lanes. I was always surprised to see so many horses used by the Germans. It seemed they were out of another war in another time. The pilots later said they hated to kill so many of those horses, but they couldn't help it. The eight heavy Browning machine guns on a P-47 can cut a horse in half. They can also cut a heavy truck in half. This ain't touch football.

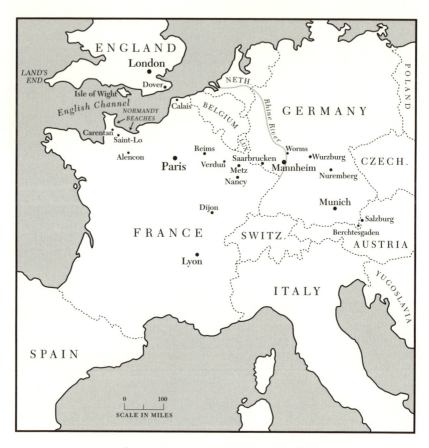

*Some of wartime Europe's familiar cities
and villages in 1944–1945.*
(*Map by Vicki Trego Hill.*)

9

On the Road Again… and Again

AFTER THE CATASTROPHE at Saint-Lo, entire German armies on the Western Front were in disarray limping out of Normandy and away from certain doom. The Americans and British moved right behind trying to catch up and encircle them. Since our squadron's mission was to provide close ground support for America's infantry divisions, we continuously moved our fighters to new strips just behind the front lines. As the bomb line advanced, so did we. The P-47s stayed in extremely close air-to-ground contact.

The 50th Fighter Group pulled up stakes at Carentan and moved quickly to three new French landing strips, the third near a little village named Meautis. The bomb line was moving twenty or thirty miles a day even though the determined Germans put up tremendous resistance for each mile. The new field was a pretty sad place and we all hoped the troops would keep moving so we could get the hell out of there. Ninth Air Force engineers built the strip in a day and a night. The whole area had seen some heavy fighting within the past few days, and you could see evidence of it everywhere. It was honeycombed with slit trenches and foxholes, which were invariably dug into the hedgerows (no, we hadn't run completely run out of hedgerows yet). As soon as we unloaded, I started looking around for a place to call home. All around the hedges you could see remnants of a terrific defense fought by the retreating Germans. There were helmets, gas masks, canteens, mess kits, clothing, and ammunition, both German and American. Empty K ration boxes were scattered all over and there were C ration cans by the hundreds. I stumbled over a dead German. Depressing as hell.

Saint-Lo was just as depressing. The Allies had completely annihilated this town. It ceased to exist after the carpet-bombing and attacks by infantry and artillery. I had seen several villages in Normandy reduced practically to rubble, but I could still see part of them remaining. Saint-Lo didn't have any rubble. It was gone. American engineers bulldozed a dirt road over the flat gray dust, and our convoy moved us to the new airstrip at Meautis. Living conditions were somewhat better than Carentan, but incessant rain was more tiresome than ever. It was still a land of apple orchards and Calvados, the fiery product the French made from all those apples. It has to be the single most lasting impression most GIs carried home with them. Calvados to Normandy is like tequila to Mexico. The farmers made apple cider from the apples, and then in some magical way they distilled it until it became downright lethal. The U.S. Army loved it, especially since they could get all the Calvados they could carry for a pack of cigarettes. I always figured the Norman economy was based on a barter setup so the farmers could exchange their liquor for life's necessities. If they banked only on selling apples by the bushel they'd probably never have made it.

As much as we bitched, this new little airstrip had a few advantages. After several nights sleeping in new foxholes in the rain, we decided it would be prudent to move into tents. It was wonderful having heavy canvas between the weather and me. The thing we didn't miss at all was the daily shelling by a German 88mm cannon (which incidentally is still considered by many to have been the best artillery piece of the war in Europe). As good as the Germans were at making war, they were unimaginative time-clock punchers. They got into the habit of shelling our Carentan location at certain hours of the day. It got so predictable you could almost set your watch by the time the first crump sounded—plenty of time to climb in your hole. The 88 would shell us every day at breakfast, lunch and supper. You wondered if they figured this was psychological warfare or were they just nuts. The best part of it was that they never hit anything of value. It was just an inconvenience of sorts. Our little spotter planes were never able to locate this gun and it has always remained one of life's great mysteries to me and my ex-buddies. The story had a fitting ending, though, because as soon as the Allies dismantled Saint-Lo our 88 artillery quickly joined the retreating Wehrmacht.

The battlefront moved so rapidly, the German armies were scattered all over Normandy. Fighter-bombers constantly severed their communications and much of the time a panzer division would have nothing more than a vague idea of where other divisions were. The P-47s were flying almost constantly, taking out bridges, phone lines and fuel dumps. So we had come a long way from that narrow strip of beachhead where the front lines were static and the German lines were intact. Now all of these massive armies began to intermingle; the battlefront was so fluid that the danger of friendly fire became a real problem. Nobody wanted to blunder into another Saint-Lo situation, so the army devised a daily color code for all our vehicles. I hope somebody got a promotion for coming up with the answer. They furnished brightly colored panels of plastic (I guess) with tie downs so they could be lashed on to the hoods of all vehicles. Color codes changed every day: one day would be a bright day-glo red. Next day all jeeps, trucks and other vehicles carried brilliant green, the next day the panels were yellow—until they ran out of colors, at which time they started all over. I believe the color panels saved a lot of lives because they said once more "Don't shoot me."

After two weeks of living in tents, most of us began to collect stuff. Anything to help make life a little homier. I found a chair in a bombed out house, brought it back to the tent and used it to sit down on and write letters home. We collected dozens of things; souvenirs, wash stands, wooden shoes, you name it. So naturally, just when we got sort of comfortable, the word came to move up, since the infantry and artillery were moving so fast. This always happens every time you move. You manage to lose or throw away a lot of things that aren't immediately useful, namely because you have to cart them around. Some of the first things GIs dumped were their gas masks. You could see hundreds of them all over Normandy. They're probably still there today under tons of horse manure.

So we struck the set and moved forward to the next landing strip at a hamlet named Lonrai. By this time the Germans were so disorganized we were able to travel in one long convoy. As we got set up to do serious business again, one of the great battles of the war began. It became known in the history books as the Battle of Falaise Gap. Two elite German armies were almost completely encircled by American, British and Canadian units near the town of Falaise. The so-called gap was forty miles long and thirteen miles wide shaped like a giant horseshoe. The Germans tried desperately to escape the circle before it closed. Some made it; most didn't. The terrain dictated that they retreat down a main road; not realizing it was studded in the hills on both sides with American artillery. The 105mm and 155mm guns had been placed some ten yards apart, and they fired thousands of rounds into the fleeing armies. In addition, our P-47s strafed them all day long. Except for shallow ditches on the roadside Germans had no place to hide. It was a bloody shooting gallery.

General Eisenhower toured the Gap on foot two days later and described it as one of the major "killing grounds" of the war. He said, "Roads, highways and fields were so choked with destroyed equipment and dead men and animals that passage through the area was extremely difficult. I encountered scenes that could be described only by Dante. I could walk hundreds of yards at a time, stepping on nothing but dead and decaying flesh."

Thirty thousand Germans died in the slaughter and 92,000 were taken prisoner. Finally, leaving Normandy behind, the Allies started overrunning France and heading for Paris. In our squadron—and I think in all American forces—there arose this feeling of great optimism. With the Germans in retreat and with new tanks and guns and planes swarming ashore in Normandy every day there seemed no way we could lose. It was the middle of August 1944.

10

Mademoiselle from Gay Paree

THE RETREATING GERMAN ARMIES made a wise decision not to defend Paris, and except for pockets of troops covering the retreat the city was wide open for liberation by the Allies. It was the last week in August and rumors were rampant that our squadron would be among the first American outfits to enter Paris.

Sure enough, the rumors were true; old Frank had lucked out again. We quickly shut down operations and got ready to pull out in a truck convoy one morning just in time to be in on the liberation of Paris. We were to be led by our pedantic executive officer, a strange little guy by the name of Captain Panek. Strange name, too, but it fit him perfectly since he would panic at the least little military glitch. He had a John Wayne complex as well. We were all lined up ready to go. Our leader, Captain Panek, sat in the front seat of the lead jeep, then stood up and looked at his watch. He raised his right arm straight up with his index finger pointing skyward and made several circular motions, then he pointed toward where he figured Paris must be and shouted,

"Let's go, men!" Just like the old 7th Cavalry. The captain couldn't see us grinning but it seemed funny as hell at the time. Our cup runneth over.

Anyway, we were off to a happy start. My friend, Schwarz, was the driver of this truck (known in the army as a six by six) and I was his only passenger—riding "shotgun." In the back end we carried a big tank of water and lots of other essentials necessary to move an army. At least we wouldn't die of thirst. About noon we stopped for lunch, hauled out the K rations and lay around on the road shoulder for a break. The road was in pretty good shape considering the devastation it suffered so recently. It had been clogged with parts of a German army, burned out tanks, trucks, artillery pieces, carts laden with the loot of France and dead horses and cattle. American engineers came through hours later and just bulldozed everything into heaps by the side of the road.

Paris was now less than a hundred miles away and we were moving along at a pretty good clip when we got an air raid alert passed along by the vehicles in front of us. Our convoy would have made a good target since we probably couldn't get off the road and we were traveling a little too close together. Somewhere along the line old Sandy had lost or misplaced his helmet (which never seemed important to him anyway). When the alert occurred, Sandy panicked a bit, having no protection for his head, and said with what he thought was perfect logic, "Hey F. J., if I'm driving and I get hit I'll wreck the truck, and we'll both die. Right? So why don't you lend me YOUR helmet?" With my usual eloquence I said, "Old buddy, what is it about the words 'Fuck You' that you don't understand?" At any rate, there was not a Luftwaffe fighter in sight that day but I always valued Sandy's logic, even fifty years later.

The farther we drove toward Paris the friendlier the people became. It was obvious that the Normans suffered more from the Germans than did the people in and around Paris. As we began to close in on our destination, folks in the outlying villages lined the streets waving and shouting and making the V for victory sign. And thereby hangs a tale so fantastic I was never able to find the words to describe it in letters home.

As soon as we hit the city limits (I assume Paris actually had city limits) people were lined solidly along the streets cheering our arrival. It was an experience I was really fortunate to have, like once in a lifetime. Everywhere people cheered, waved, shouted, and even the girls kissed us. Women ran up and gave us opened bottles of champagne, wine, cognac, flowers and fruit. Little kids ran up to our vehicles and climbed on. The GIs were throwing down packs of cigarettes, candy, gum, cans of food, and the Parisians loved it (even the Spam). They clapped and waved American flags just like a Fourth of July parade magnified a million times over. Old Sandy (who hardly needed a helmet now) and I had big beautiful flowers hung on our olive drab truck, and a cute girl came up and fastened a rose on my helmet, a big red one. Other Americans in tanks, halftracks and jeeps had lipstick smeared on their faces—and loved it, too. All the downtown buildings near the Champs-Elysees flew American, French and British flags. Where the *verboten* flags came from I'll never know. Hordes of exuberant Parisians crowded onto red, white and blue draped balconies and perched precariously on rooftops.

It looked like a movie with a cast of thousands or a TV documentary. You had to see it to believe such things happen in real life. Anybody in an American uniform was a hero in that city; and for us it was the most wonderful feeling in the world to be so highly thought of. For me the liberation of Paris had to be the most emotional day of the war. But it was not hard to understand. The French people had been beaten down for almost five years, and with emotions pent-up inside so long, they just exploded with joy and thanks.

This mass of heavy equipment and soldiers kept moving like a

khaki river through downtown Paris and slowed to a crawl as we
passed regular neighborhoods and apartment houses. The French
were still jammed ten deep in the streets. Next occurred one of
the fastest moves in the history of warfare.

A well-endowed French girl stood out from the crowd, raising
her hand and shouting "Hey GI! Hey GI!" She seemed to be
looking directly at a buddy of mine, one PFC Bill Ganey. Never
bashful, Bill held out his palms and hollered, "Who, me?"

The mademoiselle shouted *"Oui!"* I should tell you here
that Ganey was probably the handsomest GI in the European
Theater of Operations: black hair, blue eyes, and a six-foot-three
basketball player from the University of Illinois. He loved the
girls and hated the army. Seconds later Ganey was out of his
weapons carrier and in the embrace of Miss Paris. They scooted
around the corner of this apartment house, conveniently block-
ing our view of what would soon become the world's fastest
stand-up-against-the-wall sexual encounter. Within two minutes
they threaded their way back to the street, both laughing while
Ganey tried to button his pants. The two lovers waved fondly as
the parade moved on and I made a note to send this to the
Guinness Book of Records.

Well, we plowed all the way down the main drag till we got to
Orly Airport, which was the largest in Paris. The Germans had
taken it over in 1940 and used it as a major bomber and fighter
base. We were delighted to find out this was to be our new home,
even though American bombers had only recently flattened it.
Big hangers were demolished. Wrecked and burned German
planes were strewn all over the taxi strips. The huge concrete
runways were pitted with hundreds of bomb craters. But within
a couple of days army engineers moved in and quickly did some
bulldozing, filled in the craters on runways and taxi strips, and
we had a real airfield with real runways for the first time.

A number of the buildings were only partially demolished so

we had our pick of deluxe quarters. Six other guys and I moved our gear into what had been some kind of a German headquarters. We had a tough time believing such opulence still existed. After months of camping out in those Normandy foxholes this was heaven. We had this big rug on the floor, blue velvet overstuffed chairs, closets, pictures of Hitler on the wall, and cases of champagne. We were still eating K rations since supply lines were now over extended as the infantry and armored divisions moved on out of Paris (poor bastards) in pursuit of the retreating Germans. We even had running water, showers and bathtubs. But I think best of all these indoor conveniences was simply electric lights. I hadn't seen a light at night since we left England, and it was well blacked out. Ingenious, these Germans. The first thing I did was take a hot tub bath, the first for many months (even if there was a German officer bathing in it last week). Actually, I hadn't been in a bathtub since we left the States back in March.

That first night in Paris was another one of those vivid memories that become imprinted on your brain and seem to pop up out of nowhere, even today. Four of us, Schwarz, Pearce, good buddy Harry Kaiser (the tallest guy in the squadron) and I cleaned up our act. Meaning we bathed and changed into our driest and cleanest uniforms. As I recall, we just walked off the base and headed for the nearest cluster of bright lights. We didn't need no stinking badges. After we'd walked about three blocks small arms fire broke out somewhere in the neighborhood. Just as we started looking for a hole in the sidewalk to perhaps save our butts, a group of French guys and their girlfriends came by walking and singing and laughing. One girl said, in English. "No problem wees zee shooting. Eet happens all zee time!"

So the four of us all-American heroes went on our way—but feeling kind of sheepish. In fairness though, we were only a day away from ducking every time we heard something that sounded like pop pop pop. Later on as we saw more and more Frenchmen, they usually acted bullet proof unlike the brave Americains. It turned out there was the crack of small arms fire all over town. The remaining Germans were still holding out for the fading glory of the Greater Reich, and the French guerillas (bands of trigger happy young men called the FFI or Free French of the Interior) were going to make sure their former captors never got out alive. It turned out that same day in Paris 3,000 Germans were killed and 10,000 more were taken prisoner. The FFI got blamed for lots of unnecessary killings but I have always thought they played an active and brave part in liberating their country. Meanwhile, the Parisians rounded up anybody thought to have collaborated with the Germans and either beat hell out of them or executed them on the spot. Women accused of collaboration were forced to kneel down in the streets while men shaved their heads. Not a pretty sight.

My buddies and I turned the next corner and encountered the happy sound of music. We practically rushed the open front door of a family tavern, and then walked inside. The music suddenly stopped in the middle of a polka and so did the conversation. Dead still. They took one look at us, and broke into cheers. I guess we were their first Americans and they were charmed to see us in their neighborhood pub. As soon as we realized we weren't going to get mobbed, the super friendly bartender laughed like Santa Claus and shook hands with each of us. He invited us in to enjoy the festivities but first he asked us to put our carbines on top of the bar—just like the Old West. We smiled and obliged, especially since we weren't planning on shooting any Frenchmen that night.

Drinks—for us anyway—were on the house. We each had a beer and toasted the crowd. Then the live music started again. Two French guys, one playing an accordion and the other a violin struck up "La Marseillaise" and the crowd went crazy. They all stood up and belted out their national anthem with fervor and emotion the likes of which I'd never heard. I noticed many of them had tears streaming down happy faces. The Americans represented a nation that had just released them from German razor wire and they loved us, although we hadn't literally stormed the barricades when Paris got liberated. We just drove through town in a GI truck.

They fell in love with our Corporal Kaiser because he was as tall as their headman, General DeGaulle. Well, at about this point the musicians invited the crowd to dance, and so they did. Almost everybody, from little kids to grandmas got up and danced to some obviously popular French polka. The four of us got coerced into trying this strange (to us) beat. And we weren't all that bad. A good-looking brunette cut in and asked me to dance with her. I think it was the first time that ever happened to me and I, of course, was delighted. This never happened back in El Paso. As soon as that tune ended, a real cute blond cut in and we began dancing to a much slower piece, more to my liking. She was a good little dancer and she told me her name was (what else) Simone. She then advised me that the other girl I danced with was maybe sick with a very bad disease from sleeping *avec le Bosch*. The French always called Germans "Bosch" and I never really knew what it meant. I think it meant a German pig. At any rate it was definitely not a term of endearment. You would hear *"Bosch kaput"* daily when a Frenchman was telling you that the Germans were all killed or gone.

I danced with Simone most of the evening, especially since the last thing I needed was some dread social disease to take home from Paris. The evening passed so quickly it was time to close the tavern before I realized it was midnight. Simone asked me if I wanted to meet her at the cafe the next night and dance some more. I told her oui but I had guard duty that night. But how about the next night? She said, "Okay" in English. The French learned American slang real fast. Everything was beautiful; I hadn't really seen a girl up close in months, much less danced with one.

So the three other musketeers and I picked up our carbines and headed back to the base. Turns out my pals also had a fine time with all the neighbors. After midnight the streetlights turned off and we walked on in the dark. Suddenly there was this long loud burst of machine gun fire coming from what looked like a large closed garage or warehouse next to us. The four of us un-limbered our carbines wondering what the hell was going on. The answer was not long in coming as a young guy with an FFI armband came out the door to see who we were. He was de-lighted to see his first Americans. We asked him in our pidgin French what was happening in there. He lit a cigarette I gave him, made a motion with the edge of his hand across his neck and merely said, "Bosch kaput." Jesus.

The next night I did indeed pull guard duty—across the street and about two blocks from the base. Again it was after midnight (strange things seem to happen to me after midnight) and the FFI's trigger-happy guys were shooting up a storm at God knows what. I was walking guard around a big old school building the Germans had confiscated for a headquarters. It supposedly con-tained valuable military papers the Wehrmacht didn't have time to pack up when they left just ahead of us. The U.S. Army wanted to look at this stuff. Guards were instructed, "Nobody goes in or out, *compris?*" The building, by now was a disaster, with three stories of partly shattered windows and broken plaster. I heard what I thought was somebody walking around in there, so I hollered, "Who's there?" No answer, probably because nobody WAS there. Anyway the sound of small arms fire continued all around the neighborhood, and I thought, what the hell? So I proceeded to start shooting out the remaining windows. I'd al-ways wanted to do something like that. Nobody came running obviously because of the constant popping of FFI guns. I shoot out windows and nobody gets killed. Just another act of heroism.

11

Au Revoir Paris,
Back to the War

WELL, IT HAD TO END sometime. Our infantry and armored divisions were pouring northward toward the Belgian border sometimes forty or fifty miles a day. So we piled back into the six by six trucks and headed north out of Paris. It was the second week in September and Patton's Third Army had rolled all the way to Verdun before halting abruptly because of empty gas tanks. All around this part of France were the battlegrounds where millions died during the First World War: the Argonne Forest, Meuse, Rheims, the Somme, Chateau-Thierry, Belleau Wood, Nancy and others. There were hundreds of miles of timeworn and weatherworn trenches and shell holes around us where the Allies and the Germans killed and maimed each other at close range for literally years.

We settled in near a hamlet named Crepy (the GIs called it Creepy or Crappy). The engineers prepared the usual steel matting runway and the 10th began flying short fighter sweeps from there. By the time we left Orly Field at Paris we were too far from the battlefront to make these quick missions. Actually, at this new little dump we were still quite a way from the front lines so we didn't have to put up with a lot of minor inconveniences like living underground. We started living in tents; six guys to a tent. But everything was dull and monotonous and the chow remained dull and monotonous. Even your buddies seemed dull and monotonous. We just missed the element of excitement.

What happened was that the big divisions moved across France so fast they got ahead of supply lines coming from the U.S.A. and the Channel in Normandy. There was a shortage of everything; food, fuel, clothing, cigarettes, you name it. Bummer.

You got in line at the mess tent and they handed you a can of C ration beef stew, a little can of hardtack and a packet of instant coffee powder, and that was it. Sometimes the entrée would be corned beef. We heard all this canned beef came from Argentina and that seemed to make it even worse. Don't ask me why—what's wrong with Argentina? It was hard to imagine how good a hamburger would taste, or chocolate cake, or ice cream or a glass of milk. I was not real bright throughout this whole unpleasantness —I didn't drink coffee. I wasn't afraid that it would stunt my growth or anything—as people used to tell me. I just didn't care for the taste of it. Part of our K ration boxes contained a little packet of powder to make lemonade. Well, I always traded my coffee packets for somebody else's lemonade. On cold, rainy, frosty mornings these guys would stand there with water dripping off their raincoats, drinking streaming hot coffee and I would stand there shivering drinking ice-cold lemonade. I finally realized that my paycheck was commensurate with my mentality.

This northern part of France was basically pretty nice. I remember it looking a lot like Ruidoso, New Mexico. But with the incessant drizzle and two huge armies trying to blow it to bits, it was not all that beautiful. We didn't get to see many people, either. They lived in tiny villages and each little house had a huge pile of manure in the front yard. We never were able to figure this out except that probably the more manure you had the higher your social status in the community. The little kids were dirtier and more ragged and not cute like the Normandy kids. It was another wooden shoe deal. But you had to feel sorry for them. We kept all the kids well fed. They gobbled up corned beef as if it were sirloin steak. And after meal times when the cooks dumped out leftovers, all the kids came around with empty cans and scooped up everything in sight. During the years of occupation the Germans had been confiscating almost everything from the French farmers for their troops so it didn't leave much for dessert.

The war ground slowly on. Weather conditions kept the Thunderbolts on the ground much of the time so the German army held the line, quit retreating and we were now at a stalemate. Instead of the Allies moving forward thirty miles a day, we moved maybe thirty feet. We had no problems from the Luftwaffe's planes because they couldn't fly either. We mostly just sat around in wet clothes, looked at each other in the semi-darkness of a tent and watched the rainwater slowly drip on our blankets. We're talking monotonous here.

We finally got orders to move again, perhaps since we were still getting minimum wage for doing absolutely nothing. Like a bunch of Gypsies we packed up and headed for another northern France landing strip at Toul. It was no better or worse than where we'd suffered through the past few weeks. Meanwhile, another invasion was well underway, this time on the French Mediterranean Coast. It was code named Anvil. Compared to the emotion of the Normandy landings and liberation of Paris this southern invasion didn't get all that much attention from the American press—and public. But it became a major battleground in Marseilles, Toulon and other Riviera coast towns.

From Italy the Americans revitalized their Seventh Army with ten infantry divisions, many of them combat hardened troops directly from Sicilian and Italian victories. Leading the southern invasion were the 36th (Texas) Division, the 45th Division ("Thunderbirds"—including many Apache and Cherokee Indians from Oklahoma), and the famous 3rd Division from the Italian campaign. Ninety-four thousand troops landed on the southern beaches the first day and 367,000 had landed within a month. These included four Free French divisions that sailed from North Africa, as well as British and Canadian forces. The ranks of the Free French were filled with soldiers from the homeland who had fled one jump ahead of the Germans four years previously. Along with the Free French came a polyglot of volunteers from France's empire: Algerians, Tunisians, Syrians, Lebanese and others including 6,000 fierce, barefoot Berber tribesmen from Morocco with their heavily laden mules. They had almost been left behind because they refused to travel without their beloved mules. There was also official concern about their violent instincts in a place like France. For one thing, I recall they didn't take prisoners. But c'est la guerre. They showed their mettle by sealing off Marseilles from the fleeing Germans. The Foreign Legion from a dozen countries invaded along with the French.

So here we go again. Strike the tents and get the hell out of here. This time it's due south to the Rhone Valley at Lyon and this time we go by air. Who's complaining?

12

Southern France's D-Day

THE MILITARY PLAN for the Mediterranean invasion banked heavily on the U.S. Seventh Army, which along with its Allies would liberate Marseilles and the rest of the coast. Then they would drive north through the Rhone Valley and Lyon, eventually linking up with Patton's Third Army in northern France. This would liberate an immense part of France in one huge operation. Not bad thinking.

It was early October 1944. About sixty of my 10th Fighter Squadron buddies and I climbed aboard a C-47 on our runway at Toul and roared off into the wild blue yonder. These transports didn't have any of the creature comforts of, say, American Airlines. As I remember, we sat in aluminum bucket seats lined up against the sides of the plane. We piled all our gear into the center aisle. First thing I did was look for the parachutes and I could only see three. I asked one of my knowledgeable pals, "Where's the rest of the parachutes?" He said, "That's them." "You mean we've only got three chutes for sixty guys? What are we gonna do if we have to bail out or get shot down?" He grinned and said, "Pray a lot."

These C-47s weren't pressurized, of course, so we flew fairly low. Before long I had a great view of the French Alps, but along with the view we encountered extremely rough air over the foothills. Well, my associates started taking bets again as to how soon old Mangan would get airsick. They didn't have to wait long since the C-47 was bouncing all over the sky and I became terminally nauseated. The contents of my stomach were already in my throat by the time I jerked the liner out of my helmet and stuck my head into the metal part. It worked like a charm, but it had a contagious effect on lots of my so-called friends. The inside of this C-47 was a mess. We finally slid onto the runway with the wind blowing from what seemed like all directions. The plane bounced back into the air twice before we actually slithered to a stop.

The rest of the squadron and our planes followed us several days later. The mission was to fly short ground strafing and low level bombing missions up and down the Rhone River Valley to keep the Germans from escaping France. So we were now operating out of a real airport named Bron at the edge of the large city of Lyon. The field had concrete runways and hangers but most were unusable because the Allies had pretty well flattened everything with high explosives. There was wreckage of every kind of German plane scattered all around, and I had a field day photographing the swastikas and black crosses and various camouflaging. The Germans were experts with their paint schemes—their planes even looked menacing. By this time, our newest planes arrived without camouflage, just bright aluminum as they came from the Republic factory to replace P-47s lost in combat. The reason was, of course, that by then America had such air superiority that we didn't need to hide them in the sky.

I need to tell you something about the German SS, in case you've wondered. The initials stand for SchutzStaffel, which means kind of a protection group—originally Hitler's private bodyguards. Even their uniforms were intimidating; all black with silver trim to denote their rank and unit. In front line combat divisions they were known as the Waffen-SS and they wore field gray uniforms displaying the SS initials. This marking was a stylized emblem that looked like two lightning bolts, an ancient Germanic symbol of Thor the Thunder God. Teutonic knights displayed this symbol during the Middle Ages. The SS also wore a distinctive collar insignia of a silver death's head skull and crossbones. Is it any wonder they scared hell out of people? These "black knights" were trained in Nordic lore to be the elite of the Third Reich. And of all the military units fighting in World War II these bastards were by far the most infamous.

All our guys had heard of Nazi atrocities but were never sure they happened. We found out the first few days in Lyon. One of the most dreadful experiences I can recall from the entire war happened at Bron Airbase outside this lovely old city of Lyon. I witnessed the excavation of a bomb crater in which the Nazis had buried more than two hundred of their victims after first machine-gunning them. This was just one of the atrocities committed by the infamous SS officer Klaus Barbie, better known as the Butcher of Lyon. His SS troops rounded up these French Jews, lined them up on the edge of the crater and murdered them—whole families, men, women and little kids. Girls of seventeen and eighteen, guilty only of being Jewish were slaughtered here. When we arrived, French Army officers supervised captured SS troops who were made to dig down and remove the bodies. Our troops standing closer to the pit than I was said that many of the victims had been buried alive since they had dirt and sand lodged under their fingernails from scratching at the soil. As the excavation went on, other German POWs carried the bodies to the nearby ruins of an airplane hanger and placed them side-by-side on the concrete floor for final identification. And of course, the

In Lyon, the Nazi SS executed more than 200 French Jews on the edge of a bomb crater. The SS troops then bulldozed them into the crater and filled it with dirt. Some of the victims were buried alive. After we arrived, the Nazis were forced to dig up the bodies and place them in an airplane hanger.

smell of death was awful. This entire episode is still stamped on my brain. I just couldn't believe such cruelty existed even after seeing it with my own eyes.

In Lyon we lived in tents because the safety factor was so good here—the Germans were in full retreat. The climate was warmer but it still rained and drizzled day and night. Our bivouac area was nothing more than a knee-deep sea of slippery, gooey muck. It was a lot like adobe, stuck to our shoes and gathered more with each step until our feet looked like two big chunks of clay. To get in and out of the tents we rustled up some long thick boards, put them on top of bricks, and they worked just like little bridges.

In Europe there was no such thing as a day off from the war. Every day was much like the day before. You never had the fog-giest idea of whether it was Sunday or Wednesday because it really didn't matter. I never heard anybody complain about it. One reason was that everybody had a job to do and they wanted to get all this over with as soon as possible. Another reason, and a very compelling one, was what would you do with a day off? If you wandered very far away from camp you might get unlucky and get killed. And if you had some time off, who would want to spend it in one of these mud holes anyway? There were exceptions, though, like our outfit getting stuck in Paris for three weeks. These were real morale builders because it was easy to get a pass into town if you planned it right. In the parts of France that I saw, most towns were just small farm villages that offered nothing in the way of exciting recreation for the GIs. But cities like Paris—that was something else. And Lyon was something else as well. It was third in size after Paris and Marseilles, and the citizens were ecstatic when the Germans retreated from the city before the advancing Americans rolled in.

Two thousand years ago Roman legions founded Lyon and the town became part of their empire. In the Middle Ages Lyon was a good-sized city and it still has a medieval look. It sits beside the large Rhone River that is fed by snow water from nearby massive Alpine peaks. Both Switzerland and Italy are less than a hundred miles away. As I remember, the people looked much different than the French in Normandy and around Paris. In Lyon they were predominately darker skinned, with darker hair, and many of them had a Spanish or Italian look. I figured the ancient genetic pool was still at work. They also dressed differently than people in other parts of the country. Lots of men wore knickers and hundreds of people walked about the streets wearing what looked like riding breeches, heavy hob-nailed shoes, long white wool stockings, heavy sweaters and tams.

School kids were already using backpacks in 1944.

There wasn't much left standing at the Bron airport in Lyon except this one large building that had been used by German officers as living quarters. So our management team decided our pilots and headquarters could use it to get out of the rain. And I was put on the clean-up detail to make it livable again. The Germans had obviously vacated in a hurry because they left an amazing amount of junk. Wine bottles, papers, German books, magazines, uniform caps, you name it, were scattered all over the place. Every room had an immense picture of der Fuhrer hanging on the wall and a lot of them had Goebbel's picture alongside Hitler. I asked the first sergeant what we should do with all this stuff and he said, "Burn it." However, on one wall was a large, beautiful oil painting. From what little I knew about French impressionist painting, I figured this might be one of them. My plan was to carefully take it out of the frame, roll it up, and later send it back to El Paso. I could almost see the headlines at home: LOCAL HERO LIBERATES FAMOUS VAN GOGH PAINTING. So I quietly stashed it in a corner for safekeeping. We built a big bonfire in the courtyard, burning all the trash and pictures of Hitler. You guessed it. My painting was missing. I asked one GI what he'd done with the painting. He said, "The sergeant told me to throw it in the fire."

It was pretty quiet on the flight line so Pearce and I wangled passes to town. I hadn't had a bath since Paris, and that was way more than a month ago so I decided to grit my teeth and clean up my act. Since we were now so far from the front lines there was no problem with lighting a fire at night. I set the helmet full of water on a roaring fire and took a much needed sponge bath, shivering the whole time. I even washed my hair, shaved and put on a clean uniform (the kind that French women charge a pack of cigarettes to wash). It was good to feel like a human again.

Getting to town was easy because there were always GI

vehicles moving back and forth. The first truck that came along picked up Pearce and me and dropped us off downtown. We just stood around deciding what to do, when like a godsend, along the sidewalk came four nice looking French people. They turned out to be a family—mama and papa and two teenage daughters. They stopped, said *bon soir,* shook our hands and told us how happy they were to see zee Americans. We told them we were also happy since we hadn't seen many civilians for so long. We all introduced ourselves. One girl was named Monique and her sister was Suzie. The parents' name was La Fay. For all they knew we were a couple of serial killers but apparently that hadn't entered their heads. They asked us if would come to dinner at their house (but reminded us that food was hard to come by so please don't expect anything fancy).

They lived within walking distance so we set out for *la maison.* It was almost 9:00 P.M. but we found out that the French eat dinner much later than Americans. They lived in a nice, small house. I don't remember what papa did for a living but he had an office job of some sort. They also had a little sister about seven years old, and damned if she wasn't wearing wooden shoes. While mama was preparing dinner we sat around and communicated pretty well considering neither of us spoke the other's language. I pulled out my handy GI French-English tour guide and stumbled through such phrases as *Ou est la gare* (meaning where is the railroad station)? They were kind enough to laugh. Monsieur La Fay opened a bottle of red wine that we enjoyed while watching Madame La Fay make crepes suzettes in a frying pan. She only used about an eyedropper of oil, telling us it was *beaucoup* hard to get. But her cooking was a real treat for us in the Spam Circuit.

We asked the girls if they would go to the movies with us sometime. They thought that was fine, especially if mama and papa could chaperon. That was okay with us and we set a date for a few days in advance. The next time Pearce and I showed up we brought along a musette bag full of cans of beef stew, Spam, a large bottle of cooking oil, a dozen rolls of Lifesavers (which we hated), and a can of orange marmalade. All liberated from our mess tent. They were thrilled with all this yummy stuff. We did go to the picture show and laughed all the way through a 1939 Laurel and Hardy film—dubbed in French of course. The last year American films had been seen in France was 1939. Pearce and I had a great time. They made us promise to come back again, which we did several times. And yes, we would write.

With all these passes into town came a sense of foreboding. This was just too good to last. The American Seventh Army had pushed the Germans all the way up to Alsace-Lorraine and the 10th was now too far away to do much good. It was time once more to move up.

13

Wintertime in Alsace-Lorraine

After the Germans retreated from the French Riviera, Lyon, and the rest of southern France, it came as no surprise that the 10th would follow the exodus—this time almost all the way to Belgium. We convoyed up the Rhone River Valley, and the farther north we went, the more it looked like winter was about to arrive. It was early November 1944. At about noon the first day, the convoy pulled over to the side of the road and the troops piled out for chow. We opened cans of C ration beef stew, raised the hoods of all the vehicles, then set the cans on top of the hot engine blocks to warm up. At least it was a hot meal of sorts. As I recall, we opened the cans with an attached key opener. The convoy went through a few little villages, the names of which I had no idea. Then wintertime arrived with rain turning to sleet. So we just kept going long after dark. I figured we would keep driving all night fighting the sleet while slowly freezing to death in the back of the stinking truck. But no, our captain who was leading this miserable ride had planned ahead to save his troops.

About 9:00 P.M. we pulled off the main road, and the heavy vehicles groaned all the way to the top of a hill. There I saw what looked like a movie set appearing through the sleet. It was a real honest-to-God medieval walled fortress. You could see where the old drawbridge used to be. It even had a moat circling the whole thing. The convoy entered through a large archway that still had the wheels and pulleys for the bridge. Inside was the small village of Langres, which loomed through the mist like an apparition, reinforcing this whole cinematic quality. We drove all the vehicles through four of these archways before we reached the night's destination. My feet felt like they were frozen solid and I wanted to get out of the weather in a hurry. So I was the first guy off the tailgate and I jumped out instead of slowly sliding down. Well, when my feet hit the cobblestones they felt like two stumps and I crashed. Two guys lifted me up and helped me hobble inside to a warm and welcome room. I took off my shoes and massaged my feet. In a few minutes they were okay. No problema. It turns out this place had been used by lots of different medieval armies as well as modern French, Russian, German, and now American.

The Americans stationed there were part of a service company providing food and lodging for GIs passing through, and they couldn't have been friendlier. I don't know why they smiled because here it was the middle of the night and they were about to feed us a hot meal. They opened up their mess hall for us at 10:00 P.M. And surprise, no C rations—just really good eating, probably one of the high points of the war in Europe. They pointed us to their barracks and gave us each a cot and blankets and we sacked out. They didn't turn off the lights (yes, they had electricity) so I asked their sergeant if they always slept with the light on. He said, "No, I thought you all did." So they turned off the 100-watt bare bulbs hanging from the ceiling and everybody got a good night's sleep.

We drove most of the next day freezing again and arrived at our new forward airstrip in the forested mountains outside the town of Nancy. It was a good-sized town and was the industrial center of Alsace-Lorraine. The first snow of the season descended like a white curtain and by now we were not in the best of spirits as I figured this would turn out to be another Normandy—only with zero temperatures.

Through November and early December the weather dictated how many missions the 10th could fly. On lots of days the pilots couldn't find their targets because of heavy ground fog. On good days relays of four P-47s armed with bombs or rockets and flying thirty-minute shifts provided constant cover for armored or infantry units. The way it worked was that several of our pilots would be attached to ground outfits. When air to ground assistance was needed our pilot would radio his planes, and not unlike the old 7th Cavalry, they would come charging in to aid the ground troops. Stories of column cover became legend throughout our now almost halted divisions, and ground soldiers came to look skyward with admiration at the Thunderbolts. All sorts of stories abounded, like the single Sherman tank commander who radioed the flight leader of his cover, asking if the road was safe for him to proceed. "Stand by and we'll find out," came the reply. Four P-47s swept ahead and spotted three enemy tanks down the road in waiting. The pilots attacked with bombs and rockets, setting fire and destroying the German tanks.

But still the stalemate with the Germans seemed to drag on forever. One of our big problems was getting supplies. After so many months of mud and dirt most of the squadron needed warm clothing and shoes and wool caps. Cigarettes became a thing of the past. I was even getting them in care packages from El Paso. We hadn't seen anything resembling chocolate or candy except an occasional roll of Lifesavers. Food was still the same old C rations but there was plenty of it. And it wasn't just us who were

I shot these two pictures of the P-47s in the moonlight during northern France's coldest winter in fifty years. On lots of days the pilots couldn't find their targets because of heavy ground fog. On good days relays of four P-47s armed with bombs or rockets flew thirty-minute shifts providing constant cover for armored or infantry units.

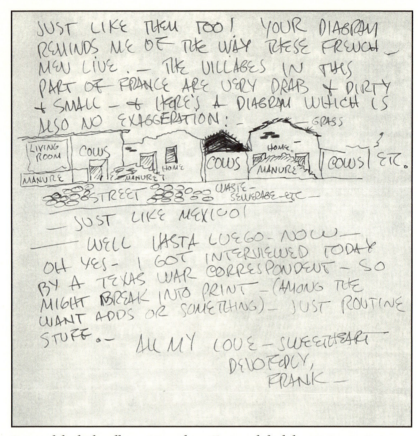

JUST LIKE THEM TOO! YOUR DIAGRAM
REMINDS ME OF THE WAY THESE FRENCH
MEN LIVE. — THE VILLAGES IN THIS
PART OF FRANCE ARE VERY DRAB + DIRTY
+ SMALL — + HERE'S A DIAGRAM WHICH IS
ALSO NO EXAGGERATION: — GRASS

LIVING ROOM | COWS | HOME | COWS | HOME | COWS | ETC.
MANURE | MANURE | MANURE
STREET | WASTE — SEWERAGE — ETC —

— JUST LIKE MEXICO!
— WELL HASTA LUEGO. NOW —
OH YES — I GOT INTERVIEWED TODAY
BY A TEXAS WAR CORRESPONDENT — SO
MIGHT BREAK INTO PRINT — (AMONG THE
WANT ADDS OR SOMETHING) — JUST ROUTINE
STUFF. — ALL MY LOVE — SWEETHEART
DEVOTEDLY,
FRANK —

*Some of the little villages in northern France defied description so in some
letters home I added a quick sketch. This one is from a letter to my mother
(who always wanted to know what it looked like over there).*

bitching our heads off. I think most of the troops in this far north
end of France were feeling shorted. Morale sagged everywhere.
At one point Dwight Eisenhower called for an investigation. It
turned out the main cause of short supplies was a thriving black
market in the Services of Supply at French ports back in
Normandy. Cigarettes and gasoline brought fabulous prices in
Paris, and some of the service troops were selling them in truck—
and carload lots. In a much earlier instance, Eisenhower himself

telephoned the rear and directed that until every forward air-field and front-line unit was getting its share of these items there would not be another piece of candy or a cigarette issued to any-one in the supply services. Ultimately, the major offenders, both officers and men, received severe sentences. In a surprisingly short time our requisitions were being promptly filled. I liked Ike.

Except for incidents like this the Services of Supply did an admirable job of keeping the troops supplied. They began sys-tems of truck transportation by taking over main-road routes in France and using most of them for one-way traffic. These became the famous Red Ball Highways on which trucks kept running continuously. Every vehicle ran at least twenty hours a day and stopped only for loading, unloading and servicing. It was known as the Red Ball Express. Its drivers were mostly black troops from the Quartermaster Corps. They shuttled back and forth in long convoys delivering massive amounts of materiel from Normandy to the front lines. As I remember, each truck had a large red ball painted on its door—a signal for other vehicles to give them the right of way (which all of us were happy to do). Vital fuel for tanks and aircraft was scarce. So was ammunition. Red Ball trucks rushed thousands of loads of heavy 105mm and 155mm shells to artillery units in front line outfits. There was no room in the trucks for winter clothing and we all still wore the uniforms provided for the June landing in Normandy. We were looking so shoddy they (I never knew who "they" were) looked in another direction for replacement uniforms. These showed up one day, all washed and pressed, from the old North African campaign. They came up through the Mediterranean and were a welcome sight, even though they were lightweight summer cotton khakis. So, most of us changed into this clothing, feeling happy to have some almost-new duds.

This new clothing issue caused some raised eyebrows, how-ever. One bright day I was riding in a jeep with another guy and we got flagged down at a crossroads. This MP walked uneasily over to the Jeep and said, "Y'all boys are out of uniform, or are you Germans?" I said, "No but my grandmother was part German." Big mistake. My companion punched me in the ribs. Our humorless MP then growled, "Get out of the jeep." We told him the replacement uniform story and that we didn't like summer uniforms either in this crazy climate. "But it's all we got." The MP looked at our dog tags, serial numbers and outfit for further checking, and we were off in a cloud of French mud. War is hell.

14

Payback Time

Early on in this narrative I described an unpleasant hassle—actually a near brawl that took place in the mess hall back in Zephyrhills. The heavy in this confrontation was a mess sergeant named Francis Xavier Hill (what a nice name for the biggest, meanest bully in central Florida). Hill was regular army and had been a roughneck in the Texas oil patch. At thirty-five or so years old he was in a squadron made up of guys more than ten years younger, many of them teenagers. There were also lots of Texans in the squadron and all of us were embarrassed when it became known that the sergeant was "one of us." On that particular day I was the object of his anger. I had just finished three bone-weary days of KP, and he put me on three additional days. I, of course, resisted and Hill, in a drunken rage, wanted to fight. That was immediately out of the question because privates don't hit sergeants, especially drunken ones. He would have been easy although I hadn't been in a fistfight since the fourth grade at Alta Vista School. They would have fried my ass for decking a soldier with three stripes. When everything eased up I checked in with our first sergeant, hoping he would do something about this extra duty. His final judgment was that I should go ahead and do the three days and forget about it. I did the three days but I didn't forget it.

When we got overseas Hill was not only dangerous, now he was armed and dangerous. He was foul mouthed, loud mouthed, a really abusive drunk who would fight with a knife or a broken beer bottle and always with someone smaller and unarmed. He was abusive to anyone he could possibly get away with abusing.

One evening my friend Schwarz had just finished eating at our outdoor field mess kitchen. He was the last one to eat and the rest of the guys had gone back to their tents. Schwarz was about to leave, his mess kit all neatly washed in the huge soap cauldrons. He noticed this kid named Bill Wroblewski who showed up hungry, tired and looking for some chow. Private Wroblewski was a small guy of Polish extraction, and Sergeant Hill didn't like Polacks either. Half drunk, as was his usual condition, he got furious at this nuisance coming when his work was nearly over. Hill shouted at him, "No more food. No more food!" The kid pleaded that he had just finished working on the flight line. He was a sheet metal worker and had legitimately been patching a hole in an airplane wing that had taken an enemy hit. The plane was scheduled to fly the next morning. Wroblewski argued that yes, it was late, but he was starving. Sergeant Hill grabbed his carbine by the barrel with both hands and swung the heavy end like a ball bat, right at Bill Wroblewski's head, hard enough to kill him if he connected. It was a lethal swing, but Hill's aim was slightly off, so luckily he didn't connect. The sergeant had missed and there was no damage done, except the kid was scared to death. It was a shattering experience and Private Wroblewski asked Sandy if he had seen the episode. Sandy said yes, he had seen it all, heard it all, and would back him up if he wanted to press charges. The next morning Sandy and Bill went to see the squadron adjutant (really the commanding officer of things that happened on the ground, not in the air). They reported exactly what had happened. The adjutant, Major Everitt Cox, made light of the whole thing. He said they were making a big deal out of nothing, that Sergeant Hill was such a good soldier, how could he have possibly done anything like that? Was Sandy sure he was not exaggerating?

After several more meetings, Wroblewski backed off, afraid of what the sergeant would do to him. Possibly kill him for squealing to the major. Sandy hung in there but told me if he'd had any sense he would have backed off too. But he knew Major Cox lived by the book, and sure enough the major conceded he had to do something about it. He dragged out his manual on Courts Martial and proceeded to have a complaint drawn up against Hill. By now old Sandy began to fear for his own life since he was now fighting alone against Hill and the U.S. Army. He began sleeping at night with his trench knife unsheathed and in his hand under the blankets. Hill was arrested.

By this time every officer and enlisted man in the squadron knew about Schwarz versus Hill. The sergeant was indeed going to be court-martialed. But some legal officers in 50th Group Headquarters felt that it would be only fair to put Hill on trial a long way from the squadron (where most of us would have been delighted to see him drawn and quartered). And here is where old Mangan enters this drama. My pal Junior, from our jeep ride on Omaha Beach, was selected to drive a jeep with Hill (unrestrained) in the passenger seat. I was to ride in the back seat fully armed and my instructions included the unsettling news that it would be my ass if Hill managed to slip away in some strange village. Our destination was to be the town of Dijon, about a hundred miles of mud south of Nancy. Dijon was a fairly large town and was the nearest U.S. Army MP Headquarters, courtroom and stockade. A couple of days later I walked over to the motor pool shortly after sunrise. There was Junior checking under the hood of the jeep making sure everything was good to go. Junior welcomed me with a big grin and told me he was real happy to see me armed with only a carbine—no machine gun this time he hoped.

He assured me the jeep was in perfect mechanical shape and I'm sure it was. But outwardly it looked like a wreck. Here was the once brand new vehicle in which we had stormed the beaches of Normandy only about eight months ago. Today, there was an ugly bullet hole in the right side of the windshield, and spreading out from the center were these jagged cracks that looked like a giant spider web. I was almost certain the destruction was caused by some careless-as-hell GI, unless the Luftwaffe had peppered the vehicle while it was out on the flight line. I've told you how muddy everything had been all winter, but the past few weeks the weather had warmed up a notch—just enough to melt a lot of the snow and create seas of soft mud. This poor jeep was completely covered with it, even on the inside. There was a lumpy glob of mud on the back end, concealing a five-gallon Jerry can of gasoline and a spare tire.

I had dim memories some years back when Fort Bliss cavalry prisoners were assigned work detail on the parade ground. Why was I, a high school student, hanging around the Fort Bliss parade ground you may ask? Answer: I used to think the horse cavalry was the most romantic branch of the army and of course Bliss was the largest cavalry post in the United States. At any rate, I became aware that the soldiers from the stockade had a large white target painted on the backs of their blue fatigues. A soldier guarded them armed with a shotgun. They used to say if you let a prisoner escape, you had to do his time, so you should go ahead and shoot him. Nobody escaped.

Then here comes Sergeant Francis X. Hill, escorted by an MP.

I was already in the back seat and Hill climbed aboard and sat in front, very sober for once. He made an effort to start a conversation, but I just didn't want to talk to the son of a bitch. So it was a fairly quiet trip to Dijon. The roads were pitiful and we had to stop once in a while to wipe mud off the busted windshield. Going through several small villages, Hill turned to me and suggested that we stop and have a cognac but he looked into the muzzle of my carbine and sadly turned away. Hill needed a drink in the worst way. He didn't show any recognition of me and I figured he was either dumber than I thought or perhaps he was trying to say let's let bygones be bygones. A little before noon we pulled up in front of the local constabulary, which had recently become American MP Headquarters, complete with courtroom and stockade. I asked Junior to shut off the motor, go inside and tell somebody we are delivering a prisoner. I didn't have to tell him to take the car keys because jeeps didn't need ignition keys. Out came Junior along with a very muscular MP who took Hill in tow and directed him to the front door. I signed the usual army paperwork and we were out of there. Old Hill looked pretty shriveled up compared to his normal bully posturing. Some people might have felt sorry for him, but I damn sure didn't. I said I wouldn't forget and I've never been real big on forgiving and forgetting. I guess it's something missing in my genetic makeup, a character flaw. I looked back and mumbled "Sayonara, you son of a bitch." I hadn't felt so good for months.

We cruised around downtown and located the American Red Cross Club and parked right in front. It seemed funny and wonderful to be in Dijon—a real city. It was a friendly place, perhaps because it obviously hadn't suffered the demolition of so much of France. I figured Dijon was where they made the mustard. It was good to see people and stores and streetcars and cafes again even for one day. Just as we got out of the jeep, people gathered around—especially little kids—to see this strange apparition in

93

their town. Neither Junior nor I had been off that airstrip for six weeks. We hadn't even seen a Frenchman, just snow and mud. We still had mud caked two inches thick on our boots and clothing. To make matters worse, I had a month's growth of beard all over my face. While the kids all inspected our ugly windshield bullet hole, we scraped most of the mud off our shoes and went inside the club for coffee and donuts. It was a beautiful place. Inside it looked to me like an ancient chateau or something. It was full of WACs, nurses, and GIs, all neatly dressed. The GIs wore ties and dress blouses. I guessed we must have wandered back into General Patton's Third Army. The Red Cross girls fed us donuts and coffee, and insisted that we take a bag of fresh donuts to eat on the road. This whole episode was like a one-day vacation with pay and besides; we got rid of Sergeant Hill, hopefully forever. Such a deal.

15

Battle of the Bulge

Aʟᴛʜᴏᴜɢʜ ᴛʜᴇ Aʟʟɪᴇs had moved through France ahead of schedule, most supplies were still coming all the way from Normandy. To unload the constant arrival of freighters from America we needed another, closer port. And that port was Antwerp, Belgium. By autumn 1944 Canadian, British and American divisions had overrun the city as well as other Belgian towns, and the American 82nd and 101st Airborne Divisions were already fighting in Holland. This campaign was code named Market Garden. It got ugly from the very beginning. And before the Allies won the battle, the British 1st Airborne Division was decimated. Only one fourth of the troops in the entire 1st Airborne survived.

Even though it was wintertime at our airstrip outside of Nancy there were enough clear days for a rejuvenated Luftwaffe to strafe Allied positions. This was the strongest attack they had made against us in several months. The German pilots concentrated on American forward airfields attempting to disable and destroy the P-47s. They had only limited success before the weather shut them down in December.

On December 16, 1944 the Wehrmacht launched a massive counter attack in northern France and Belgium. It took the Allies by surprise, although Eisenhower and his generals had been expecting some sort of a move by the Germans to recapture the Belgian port of Antwerp and put the Allies out of business. The huge counter attack would be the largest battle in western Europe and quickly became known as the Battle of the Bulge. It got its name when the Germans pushed a "bulge" fifty miles deep into the American front line in the Ardennes Forest. It was to be Hitler's final effort to defeat the Allies, an attack of desperation. He gambled a huge part of his army in the snows of northern France and Belgium. The Germans attacked with twenty-four divisions. That's a lot of men and machines when you consider that each of these divisions had some ten to sixteen thousand troops.

German commando teams, trained in sabotage and infiltration had a devastating psychological effect on us. These commandos spoke perfect English and they came through the American lines driving captured jeeps. They wore American uniforms taken from American prisoners and the Germans even had fake IDs. It was next to impossible to tell them apart from the average GI and they were doing a lot of damage, including switching road signs. A number of American convoys turned in wrong directions and went miles out of their way before discovering the sabotaged signs and stumbling into waiting enemy gunfire. These German commandos were real pros, so much so that we received orders to double the security. In our case it meant stopping and questioning anyone you didn't recognize on or near the airstrip. We were supposed to ask them questions that perhaps only an American could answer: such as "Who won the last World Series?" Or "Who is Donald Duck?" I was gun shy about questions such as the

World Series winner. If somebody asked me that question, I would have asked, "Who was playing?" Or some other dumb answer assuring an MP that I wasn't a real American.

The Germans also had a creative method of camouflaging themselves in that deep mountain snow. They wore snowsuits and white sheets or white mattress covers over their uniforms, blending in with the forest. Americans did much the same. Some ground troops ordered snowsuits quickly made in Holland. These white outfits were complete with hoods attached to cover helmets, giving the added benefit of an extra layer of clothing—a welcome item in this icebox. I don't recollect what the enemy did to help conceal their vehicles. But I do know many American ground troops used white paint on the hoods of jeeps and even on tank turrets. Many also painted their pup tents white so the tents could hardly be seen from the air. But being seen by the Luftwaffe became less and less of a problem. By the middle of December when the Germans launched this huge battle, air cover for our troops by the P-47s became a myth. This was a real no-fly zone, only because of the weather, which continued to deteriorate, snow reaching two and three feet deep. The planes seemed to huddle quietly under the pine trees, and the rest of us just huddled quietly in the tents. Outside the tents lay snowdrifts of five feet. The temperature hovered at zero most of the time—frequently it was below zero.

But all was not lost. On the day before Christmas the sun came out, burned off the constant ground fog, and it quit snowing. We were back in business and not a moment too soon as the Germans continued attacking in the Ardennes Forest. It definitely wasn't "Beginning to Look a Lot Like Christmas" except maybe for the snow, which had been on the ground for two months. Pearce and I had been living in the 10th photo tent and we decided to put up a Christmas tree. I bundled up and hiked through the forest looking for a little tree. In about five minutes I spotted the

perfect tree—a fir about three feet high. As I got closer I spied a
rusty American helmet from World War I and it had a rusty bullet hole in it. The perfect souvenir. As a collector of memorabilia
(junk to some people) I had always wanted one of these. The
British army still wore this same "tin hat" design (you probably
know what they look like). The American army wore these until
after Pearl Harbor. Just as I was about to pick up the helmet I
remembered one of those boring army training films about enemy booby-traps. It showed graphically a soldier picking up a
war souvenir and getting blown to smithereens. I wasn't going to
be that stupid so I figured I'd find an old tree limb, stand some
distance away and snag that rusty helmet. And if it was booby-
trapped I'd be out of the line of fire. Not real bright either,
because I remembered the film cautioned you that the Germans
were diabolical with these things. They would set the explosion
to go off not at the souvenir site but about five feet away as you
hooked it with your tree limb. So what to do? As much as I wanted
that helmet I figured I'd better leave well enough alone and go
chop down that fir with my Knife, Trench, M-1. I did just that
and carried it back to the tent, wondering if I was just being
chicken. I wonder about it to this day and I'll bet money that
helmet is still there from 1918.

Pearce and I decorated our tree with odds and ends and it
looked pretty nice. We sliced tin foil from film cans into strips
and made tinsel. We used gold colored foil from champagne
bottles for little bells. Most of our guys didn't even realize it was
getting so close to Christmas, and then bang it was gone. I didn't
get one package or a letter although some of the boys did. We're
talking homesick here.

We did open a bottle of cognac to stimulate a little Christmas
spirit. But about halfway through the bottle, our ack-ack started
booming and the Luftwaffe was overhead. We left the tent and
started running to the nearest hole, which was less than forty

feet away. About half way I tripped on a steel tent peg and took a swan dive into six inches of melted, icy snow. My helmet went one way and my carbine the other and I was so furious and frustrated I couldn't even get up. I just lay there thinking how much I hated Hitler.

Several serious events made history around Christmas. The American 101st Airborne Division was bottled up, completely surrounded and rapidly running out of ammunition in the town of Bastogne, Belgium. This was the besieged town where American General Anthony McAuliff replied "Nuts" when notified by the Germans to surrender. Finally, with the good flying weather more than two hundred C-47 cargo planes dropped tons of food, ammunition and medical supplies into Bastogne. Thunderbolt fighter-bombers protecting the cargo planes helped break up the German encirclement by using napalm, fragmentation bombs and machine gun fire. General Patton's 4th Armored Division also arrived and battled its way into the desperation of Bastogne. Its tanks blasted the German stranglehold, and then joined the thankful paratroopers in a linkup that finally broke the siege of Bastogne.

Earlier, the tiny village of Malmedy, also in Belgium, contributed to one of the bitterest memories of the Battle of the Bulge. Over a hundred outnumbered Americans uneasily surrendered to a large column of German SS troops. As the GIs stood there bunched up in a small pasture with their hands raised, the Germans opened fire with machine guns. There were only several survivors, and they later said that the Germans rolled on by, laughing and having a good time and taking random shots at the dead and dying Americans. Word of the massacre spread rapidly through American ground units and many vowed they would no longer take prisoners wearing SS uniforms. Shortly after Malmedy a group of German SS men were captured wearing American uniforms and were quickly executed by a firing squad.

The Battle of the Bulge was, for my outfit, more of a battle against the elements than anything else. Air cover for our troops by the P-47s became a myth. The planes seemed to huddle quietly under the pine trees and we huddled quietly in the tents. Snowdrifts were five feet deep. Temperature hovered at zero, and a dense white fog covered almost everything.

This grim Battle of the Bulge lasted some six weeks and continued until the end of January 1945. A desperate Hitler finally ordered his troops out of the tip of the bulge, at last giving up his immense counter attack as a lost cause. He paid a stiff price for his gamble, about 100,000 casualties. But America also paid a price of some 80,000 casualties. It has been justifiably called the greatest American battle of the war.

Time passed painfully slow in Nancy. The planes kept flying missions, strafing German troops as they retreated slowly back toward Germany and the Rhine. Much of the deep snow melted and our camp and flight line turned once more into a sea of mud, miring down jeeps and legs. German fighter planes reappeared as the weather cleared, and hundreds of German troops were

Shown at left is a buddy of mine named H.B. Lawson from upper New York State. Sitting around in our cold snowy tent Lawson kept telling us the first thing he planned to do when he got back home was to take his girlfriend on a camping trip. Some of us figured he'd gone nuts, and others said it was just shell shock.

still in the neighborhood struggling to get out of this hellhole named Ardennes.

We still pulled double guard duty even though things had quieted down. Once about midnight I was pulling guard near the flight line, standing under a spruce tree and slowly freezing to death. Even though it wasn't snowing, with this typical, dense ground fog you couldn't see ten yards. Then I heard what sounded like carefully placed footsteps in another group of bushes. I cautiously took my trusty carbine off my shoulder and loudly called, "Halt, who goes there?" Nothing. Then the footsteps started again. (As I remember, the army manual said you're supposed to repeat this question three times and then shoot. So that's what I did. I could hear footsteps scampering away in the fog, so I fired twice more. Nothing. So what the hell am I supposed to do? The answer came quickly with a jeep carrying the Officer of the Day and the Sergeant of the Guard. The lieutenant yelled, "What the hell's going on out here?" The sergeant came up shining a flashlight in my face (another good way to get killed). I explained the treacherous-sounding footsteps, after which we all went through the fog to those dark bushes. There were the footprints. The lieutenant said, "Hell, Mangan, it was just an animal or something. You probably shot a damn cow." With that, he and the sergeant slithered through the mud back to the jeep mumbling to themselves.

The rest of my tour of duty ended about 2:00 A.M. and sure enough the next day a French farmer shows up complaining that zee Americans shot one of his goats. However, only one bullet grazed the goat and it was not in serious condition. So we loaded the Frenchman down with all the Spam and C ration beef stew he could carry and he said okay and *merci* and wandered off. C'est la guerre.

16

Hey monsieur, you like ham? We got Spam.

IN NANCY IT WAS BUSINESS AS USUAL as the mind-numbing insanity of the Battle of the Bulge slowly became history. Blue skies again brought out the P-47s to clear the way as the Allies turned their attention toward the Rhine River and Germany itself. With occasional interruptions of bad weather the battle-tested ground-air teams worked with their usual efficiency. The Thunderbolts dive bombed communication systems, attacked German columns on the roads leading toward the Rhine, reporting every move the enemy made. German prisoners caught up in their nightmare of retreat complained bitterly about the failure of their Luftwaffe and the terror and destruction caused by our fighter-bombers. German soldiers in the Ardennes were literally surrendering by the tens of thousands. Their units could no longer communicate with one another. They were running out of ammunition and hope. And there was always the haunting reality that even if they made it back to Germany, the Russian front was closing in. Would they rather be taken prisoner by the

Russians or the Americans? It was no contest. The Russians would have jumped at the chance to execute them on the spot.

Close to our camp the army engineers hastily constructed a temporary prison made only of chain link fence topped with razor wire. It was an open-air enclosure about the size of two football fields. One night I remember seeing new POWs being herded into this mass of humanity with only the clothes on their backs. Some were fortunate enough to be wearing those heavy, ankle-length German army overcoats. Most were not so lucky. The temperature hovered at about ten degrees and the wind chill probably brought it down to zero. To keep from freezing, hundreds of them were running slowly or walking around the field's perimeter all night long. There were a few bonfires made from logs and tree branches tossed over the fence by MPs. It was a gloomy picture; these poor bastards were freezing, some were wounded, and all were understandably in a state of shock. Temporarily, there wasn't much that could be done. They were hungry and had to be fed. According to the Geneva Convention, prisoners of war should be given the same type of rations their captors ate. Well, there was one thing the U.S. Army had plenty of. And that was C rations. That's what they got to eat. They were so hungry they didn't think of accusing America of cruel and unusual punishment. At least they were forced to eat the same crap we ate.

I don't want to leave you with the thought that Americans were maniacs who enjoyed the plight of these Germans. We really didn't. But what could you do with these people? The American army was stretched thin itself. This big "holding pen" was temporary and was used only a few days at a time. So there was no need to write your congressman. The only inhumanity here was the freezing cold and the C rations, and the Americans shared these conditions with the Germans.

The next thing I did was get a jeep and scout around the nearby farms looking for something to cook. I spotted a farmhouse sitting beside a big potato patch. My jeep driver was a guy from southern Louisiana who spoke Cajun French as his first language. He and this potato farmer had instant communication although the Frenchman told me our guy talked funny. At any rate, we made a deal; the farmer would let us have as many potatoes as we wanted in exchange for enough Argentine canned beef to get him through the winter. The only catch was that the spuds were in the ground and we would have to dig them up. No problemo. We had lots of muscle sitting around in tents. These guys would love digging potatoes. They always told you never to volunteer, but I broke the rule in this big swap off. I got ten other GIs to go with me carrying picks and shovels, and we drove to the farm. The farmer was delighted with our deal, obviously because it had been months since he'd eaten any beef. "Hey monsieur, you like ham? We got Spam."

He provided us with pitchforks and other tools that made it easier to dig up potatoes. So we started digging, and it was easy because the ground was soft. We dug about a ton of beautiful potatoes, loaded them on weapons carriers, and drove back to the airstrip where the troops welcomed us as instant heroes. We ate boiled potatoes, baked potatoes, French fries, you name it. And this, mixed with the canned beef was like a miracle. We also foraged around the countryside and made deals for carrots and turnips and other yummy stuff.

Things were really looking up in the old ETO (European Theatre of Operations). The Red Ball rolled in with our winter issue of clothing. And not a moment too soon. Probably the best things were tall rubber galoshes. All of a sudden you had dry feet. We got wool socks, new long johns, new jackets that were supposed to be windproof, waterproof, and tearproof. We also got sleeping bags (which never really worked for us). They had zippers and hoods but once you got zipped up it was hell getting out in an

emergency. It was funny watching these full sleeping bags standing on end and bouncing around the area like a sack race.

Even with the new food and warm clothes I was getting psychologically weary about this time. Nothing much was happening. The
pilots were flying missions across Alsace-Lorraine into Germany
and across the Rhine, so the bomb line moved miles away. About
the only way you could tell there was a war on was at night the
horizon would light up and you could hear the far off rumble of
artillery, like a faint thunderstorm. Not that I could complain,
but life got pretty boring. I remember writing to my mother (like
most mothers she worried about me all the time) and telling her
it was safer around here than Juarez Avenue on Tuesday night.
We were processing thousands of feet of gun camera film every
day and most of it was really good. It looked just like film clips
you've seen on TV where a building or a German tank came
into view. Then the white golf balls of tracers headed toward the
target, and in a couple of seconds white clouds of fire erupted
as the .50-caliber rounds from eight machine guns exploded.
Every day we sent the newest combat film to Group Headquarters for evaluation. And they, in turn, would relay the results ahead
to the infantry and armored divisions; good intelligence for the
ground armies to know what was ahead—or behind them.

Meanwhile, a couple of things happened that brightened
my personal gloom. First, the squadron posted a notice "to all
personnel" that Mangan was now a sergeant, meaning that KP
immediately became a thing of the past, an unfond memory. I
was itching to find some sergeant's stripes to enhance my ego.
But where do you get stuff like this? Certainly not in the town of
Nancy, France. So I was sort of incognito for a while, but finally
found stripes somewhere and paid a nice lady a few Invasion
Francs to sew them on. Yea.

The next blessing was that the Ninth Air Force finally got around
to sending me a full shipment of photo supplies. Greatest of all

was a four by five Speed Graphic camera, the type I learned on in photo school back at Lowry Field, Colorado in 1942. Pearce and I and Comito could now shoot practically the whole war; combat damage to airplanes, roadside carnage after the pilots strafed retreating German troops, everything we should have been doing all along. We took record shots of things like medal presentation ceremonies to send to hometown newspapers. Colonel George Kiser presented several Purple Hearts one day. He pinned a Purple Heart on a pilot who took a nasty gash along his whole upper arm from German ack-ack. Shrapnel from a German 88 also wounded one of our armorers who also earned a Purple Heart. Two sergeants received Bronze Stars. We were now down to only two of the fifty original pilots from Zephyrhills. All the other pilots were replacements, and seemed to be getting younger as I felt older. Colonel Kiser was still there in 50th Group Headquarters, but not flying.

Finally it was early springtime and as the weather warmed up it was not unusual to see cows grazing on new grass. They would stay just off the steel runway matting between the P-47s. These pastoral scenes seemed kind of incongruous as American infantry and tanks rolled across the French border into Germany and took the major metropolis of Cologne. Americans essentially destroyed the city and the only thing left standing amid the smoking rubble was Cologne's thirteenth century cathedral. Several Ninth Air Force fighter squadrons set up shop in western Germany while we sat back there in France waiting to move on and get the hell out of our mud hole. Meanwhile, American troops were bursting into slave labor camps and freeing thousands of people. These were mostly from central Europe; Poles, Russians, German Jews, Romanians, Czechs and Bohemians. The prisoners had worked for the Nazis in various armament factories in the Ruhr Valley. They were on starvation diets, but the Germans fed them just enough black bread and soup to keep them alive and working as long as possible for the Reich. At any rate, in the spring of 1945 hundreds of these people just wandered away and began walking toward safety. They were called DPs (displaced persons). A number of them came into our camp looking for food. We fed anybody who showed up, and many of them wanted to stay and work for us—for food and protection. So all of a sudden we had a bunch of grateful, willing guys to do all the KP and shit details around the airstrip. They kept telling us it was easy work. We gave them castoff clothing, but not enough to make them appear to be American soldiers (for their own protection). We didn't want anybody else to get shot for impersonating a GI. One of these Poles told me our C rations were the best food they'd had in five years.

17

Tour de France

IN SPITE OF MY EXHAUSTION from sheer boredom in Alsace-Lorraine, living conditions improved as the weeks dragged slowly on. Except for the mud, life was better than those Normandy airstrips where you had to live underground most of the time. Now I was living pretty comfortably in spite of the weird weather. One day it would be spring like and the next day there was new snow on the ground. So Pearce and I built a shack big enough for our bedrolls, gear and duffle bags. We made a frame out of runway matting and covered it with German tarpaper. Fortunately Pearce was studying to be an engineer, so I just handed him the materials we scrounged and I raved about his prowess. We found a little tiny stove which kept the place real comfortable no matter how cold it got outside. We never worried about firewood because there were acres of it in the forest right outside the shack.

It's a funny thing about the American GI. Wherever he goes, he always improvises ways to make living easier. It's almost as though he shares something in his genes with other GIs. Every time we moved in the ETO we had to start from scratch. In a way, it was fascinating to see how quickly you could push the American gracious living button. Some temporary quarters were amazingly comfortable and in a lot of respects we lived better than the French civilians in their wartime conditions. At times you couldn't accomplish much because the moves were so frequent. But usually after pulling in to a new location, it was no more than two or three days till some of the lads had built a shack or dugout with a roof. They quickly furnished it with overstuffed chairs, rugs, stoves and cooking utensils. And the beauty of it was that you didn't have to be careful with the furniture. You could walk all over the rug with muddy feet, knowing that in a couple of weeks you'd have to discard it and start all over someplace else.

And just when I thought I'd never enjoy the luxury of a real bath again, the squadron was put on notice that we were next in line for a major hot shower. The deal was that a big trailer—like a double wide—was hauled in to the outskirts of Nancy. It seemed like the entire Ninth Air Force showed up for the event, since our squadron wasn't the only one living in the nearby pine forests. Inside the trailer were several dozen showerheads, bright heat lamps powered by a portable gasoline engine, hangers for your clothes, piles of olive drab bath towels, dozens of cakes of strong soap, and wooden planks to stand on while dressing. The shower water was luxuriously warm and each guy had about five minutes or more to enjoy it before the next one moved in. It's funny how fantastic this water felt, and I'm sure it affected most of the others much the same way. We just put our heads under the showers and let the water pour down all over us. It was really something special, particularly since it had been months since any of us had a bath. By this time I'm sure we probably smelled about like your average French civilian. We're talking morale boosting here.

Most P-47 pilots
returned safely from
strafing missions—even
with major flack damage.
P-47s sometimes came
back from combat shot
full of holes, their wings
tattered. Bottom picture
shows a French P-47 that
limped in to our landing
strip. The French pilot
was a sergeant.

Some of my colleagues were finally getting seven-day leaves and as they returned it was easy to see the change in them—like bright and cheerful. Some of them had a week in London and others went to Scotland. They said that before leaving the continent a quartermaster outfit issued them new clothes, even the new Eisenhower jackets, wool shirts and ties and new shoes. They figured the army wanted them to look like real soldiers for a change.

My turn came soon enough, and I was so eager to get out of there, I didn't wait for a buddy to team up with. I was still pretty clean after that bath, so I unpacked my best wrinkled uniform (I later got it pressed in Paris). Anyway Paris is where I headed—on the train right from Nancy. GI traveling was great, since train rides were free to soldiers. And when you got to your destination there were always GI trucks coming and going everywhere and they would pick you up in minutes. I was talking to a couple of other soldiers on the train and they said they were also going to Paris but they didn't have passes. I told them Paris was crawling with MPs picking up dozens of other guys without passes. They weren't too worried until I mentioned that under wartime rules they were not just AWOL, they were deserters. "Oh, really?" "Yes, really." "Jeez." Hours later when the train pulled into Paris my new friends jumped off and strode away happily in the direction of the bright lights. These guys were so pleasantly dumb, I had a feeling they would make it okay and get back to their outfit before they were missed.

The first thing I did was locate the familiar American Red Cross Canteen. It was full of GIs, of course, but it felt like civilization again—perhaps one of the few places in Europe where you could get real American donuts and coffee and talk to an American girl. Were American girls really that pretty? An unqualified yes. The friendly Canteen girls pointed me toward the brightest lights. Nighttime Paris was beautiful now, compared to what it looked like when we rolled in during the wild liberation six months ago. Then there were few lights and almost no vehicles except American, British and French army trucks and millions of cheering people. I began to wish I'd brought a buddy with me because I was starting to feel a little lonesome in this sea of khaki. So I headed on back to the Red Cross. "Yes, we have a room for you with about the only hot water showers in Paris." Friendly, these Yanks.

I picked up the key and went on up to my room. There was a real bed, with real sheets and real pillows. You can't imagine how it felt to stretch out on that soft bed—sheer luxury. This was the best thing that happened to me since the trailer shower in Nancy.

The next morning after free coffee and donuts, I retrieved my musette bag, which I had loaded with goodies before leaving camp, and headed toward Orly Airfield on the outskirts of Paris. Close to Orly, in the tiny town of Athis Mons, was the little café where a group of us doggies enjoyed our first night in Paris on liberation day. And here I was meeting Simone LaCroix, my dancing partner and new French girlfriend. Downtown on the main drag a GI in a jeep picked me up in minutes and let me out at Orly. The changes that had taken place since we first set up shop there in August were amazing. The army filled all the hundreds of bomb craters on the runways and repaved everything in sight. Planes of all sizes and shapes lined the rest of the field. Orly was now a major airbase for large transport planes.

Simone looked pretty cute, a little blond who really seemed to like zee *soldats Americains* (at least better than the Germans, which she said she wouldn't go out with). We had this large abrazo and everything was fine. We sat down at a table inside the café, had a cup of coffee, two glasses of vin rouge and some extremely tasty cheese sandwiches. No meat, since all of France was still on a wartime diet. But that cheese sandwich, with fresh lettuce and tomatoes, generously slathered with Dijon mustard on fresh French (what else) bread was a major treat for me after all these months in the Spam circuit. I also asked for French fries, but they just looked puzzled. Never heard of them. The little café—it had a name but it's long forgotten—was real charming, just like you would expect a charming little French café to be. It was filled with the locals, the lunch crowd. Since I was the only soldier in the place the customers all smiled broadly and gave us a toast with their vin rouge. Damn decent I thought. Yet after all, because of this Yankee invasion these good burghers were beginning to live all over again. God bless 'em.

Two nice looking middle-aged Frenchmen came over to our table and asked me—in good English—how things were going in the Ardennes. I started to say that I hadn't talked to Eisenhower in several days about the war. But common decency deemed that I shouldn't be a smart ass because these were really nice gentlemen. I answered by saying merely, "Bosches kaput."

This little village-neighborhood, Athis-Mons, was about ten miles from downtown Paris and it had sort of a rural personality. Simone and I said *au revoir* to the locals and began walking down one of the country lanes. I noticed a farmer's field next to the path and in the middle was a big haystack. I'd always fantasized spending the afternoon with a French girl in the middle of a French haystack in the middle of a world war. When I was growing up I read every adventure pulp magazine I could lay my hands on, like *War Birds, G-8 and His Battle Aces, Battle Birds* and the others that flooded the Depression market. I especially liked World War I stories about Spads and Fokkers that I could trade with other twelve-year-old boys. My favorite plots were those about American pilots shooting down three-wing-Fokkers. Then later one of the brave American heroes would meet this lovely French girl and they, of course, would spend the rest of the day in a haystack.

Meanwhile, I steered Simone in the direction of the haystack I spotted. She didn't seem to have any problem with that so we climbed up and spent all afternoon there. I should level with you and point out here that romantic Mangan never got past the hand holding stage that day. After an afternoon of intense research into the social mores of French girls I concluded that most of those ooh la la stories you've heard about American soldiers and French girls is sheer bull, wishful thinking dreamed up by other GIs to impress you with their machismo. It turns out most French girls are pretty much like their American counterparts. The French are usually raised in strict Catholic families and they adhere to the party line. As I mentioned earlier, there's no need to thank me for this sociological research.

It was getting late in this warm, sunny afternoon and the war seemed like a bad dream far, far away. But I figured I'd better start looking for a ride back to the Red Cross Canteen and my room with the white sheets. So I walked Simone back to her home, said hello and goodbye to Mama, and handed out half my Life Savers and other GI favorites. Then, with a brief goodbye to Simone and promises to write, I waved and took off toward downtown Paris feeling good.

Originally, I planned to catch the free train and go down to Marseilles and the beach towns like Nice and Cannes. I was always looking for someplace to swim but the European Theater of Operations didn't offer much, besides being too cold for comfort. However, here was an opportunity. I could jump into the Mediterranean wearing my olive drab shorts. Honest to God, this freedom of movement was a heady feeling, and besides it wasn't even illegal.

But then I figured what the hell, I'll go on back to Lyon. I still had my musette bag half full of standard American staples and I knew all along that Lyon was where I should go. At least I knew somebody there. So the next day I hitched an easy ride to the Gare del Est and caught a free train heading toward Lyon, about 250 miles south. The conductor pointed me to an old fashioned chair car containing a polyglot bunch of cutthroats, all armed to the teeth and speaking different languages. The heavy smell of garlic and sweat permeated the air. I fantasized this might be the Orient Express and if I didn't get off at the right stop I might wind up getting shot by a terrorist in Istanbul. Now heading south, every time the train stopped, my wicker-seated chair car continued to fill up with an even greater collection of races. There were French soldiers, four English Tommies, five Senegalese from French West Africa with healed scars running down both cheeks. They were all extremely tall and thin and sort of blue-black. And the red fezzes on their heads added another four or five inches to their height. In later years you could have pegged them as an NBA basketball team or maybe extras from the filming of *Casablanca* There were two Arabs in yellow turbans and long red silk robes. I found myself wondering when these guys had their last bath.

Also on board were four Russians, two of them soldiers and two were civilians. The soldiers wore green uniforms with red stars on their caps. One of the Russian civilians could speak pretty good French and with my recent submersion into the language we began to talk across the aisle. This guy was from Vladivostock, had been a prisoner of the Germans and forced into a slave labor battalion in France. He told me he had escaped and joined the Maquis (guerillas) in the French mountains and claimed to have killed lots of German soldiers with his bare hands. And who was I to argue? He had a bullet hole in his shoulder you could have dropped a dollar in. He looked like one of those Slavic characters that ate toothpaste for breakfast—about as scary as the West Africans. But he told me he liked Americans because we "killed many Bosches." I assured him that I also planned to kill many Bosches as soon as I got back to camp. The other Russian was a woman who had also escaped from a German slave labor camp and joined the underground. She looked pretty beat up too, with a long ugly scar on her right arm. She said she was from Moscow and that when she and her Russian friend got off the train they were going into Germany to raise more hell with the Germans.

I was the only American in the coach and was beginning to feel stupid for not bringing a buddy along. But I figured I could count on the Tommies if there was an insurrection on board. The British guys just sat there quietly minding their own business so all I did was say hello. I'm thinking Jesus, this is a vacation?

We finally pulled into Lyon and I and about half my coach friends got off. First I checked in at another Red Cross headquarters, which was much smaller than the one in Paris but still a welcome sight. The sound of American English was reassuring. From there I phoned Monique La Fay, my other French girlfriend (I was getting to be a real social animal, like a sailor with a girl in every port. I never did this good in El Paso). Monique invited me over for supper and I could already taste the crepes suzettes. The family greeted me warmly like old home week. I emptied out the stuff I had brought from camp, including two packs of cigarettes for Papa, who was most gracious. Cigarettes were always better than money in purchasing power. We took in a French movie that evening, then with Monique as a guide, I spent the next day sightseeing.

From downtown Lyon I could easily see the snow capped peak of Mont Blanc, at 16,000 feet the highest mountain in the Alps. We checked out a lot of medieval architecture and castles that dated back to the tenth century. Later I took the whole family out to dinner at a nearby café that was wartime pricey but what else did I have to spend money on? And besides, they heard all Texans were rich.

Next day I bid the La Fays goodbye while Monique and I pledged our undying love and promised to write even *apres* la guerre. I caught the next train heading north; rode up to Dijon where I hoped ex-sergeant Hill was still in the stockade. Then on to the mountains and home to Nancy. It was not bad getting back because that's where all my friends were. But that whole past week had done wonders for my attitude. Life was good.

18

Watch on the Rhine

Back in dear old Alsace-Lorraine things were finally picking up momentum. American ground troops continued pouring into western Germany, fighting to get a foothold for an assault on the Rhine. And here was the 10th, a million miles from the action, all of us in the squadron anxious to head into Germany. The local natives were restless and not overly friendly since their homeland bordered on Germany. For hundreds of years Alsace-Lorraine changed ownership over and over between the French and the Germans. After the French Revolution the Alsatians were at least French in spirit. Germany took control in 1871 for about sixty years after the Franco-Prussian War.

After World War I the French regained the territory until the beginning of World War II when Germany moved back in to what Hitler proclaimed as part of the Thousand Year Reich. But in 1945 the Allies drove the Germans out of Alsace-Lorraine and France again took control. I'm convinced the ancient French saying "Give a German a gun and he will march toward France" had its roots in Alsace-Lorraine.

I remember going through these villages where most of the streets had German names like Wilhelm Strasse or Kaiser Strasse. You knew those citizens weren't on your side and you seldom saw a V for victory sign because many families proudly claimed German ancestry. During World War I this whole northern part of France suffered through four years of miserable trench warfare. At various times I looked at the scars of hundreds of miles of those old trenches and thousands of shell holes that were still evident in 1945 and I'm sure they are to this day. Nature had softened these historic battlefields—like Verdun, Reims, Chateau-Thierry, and the Marne so that the ground undulated like rounded ocean waves. Horses and cows grazed contentedly on these grassy mounds that were once murderous barbed wire entanglements and seas of mud in no man's land.

By early April 1945 it became clear to the head office that if the 50th Fighter Group was to keep up the hourly and daily pounding of Germany, we should move to Germany. So like Gypsies, we happily struck the set again, mounted up and headed for the nearest town, which was Metz, in Alsace. Metz was a city of about one hundred thousand people, only fifty miles from the German border. So you can imagine the non-cheers that greeted us as our loaded convoy groaned down Main Strasse. It seemed nearly all the street signs had German names. The citizens were now returning. Most of them had wisely left town when General Alexander Patch's U.S. Seventh Army (to which we were now assigned) fought its way through this area. Metz fared pretty well considering. Nothing like the pile of rubble that was Saint-Lo. Lots of shops reopened and we used a chow break to check it out. It was an ancient place, with a number of great looking castles right out of the Middle Ages in the center of town.

Next stop, Saarbrucken, just across the border in Germany. It was smashed even flatter than those French towns back in Normandy. There wasn't much left of it except piles of brick and stone and smashed cars and we convoyed over the top of the rubble on a path cleared by the engineers. It was a graveyard. The only sound was that of our trucks and other vehicles grinding through in low gear. You wondered where all the people went and it was difficult not to feel sorry for those civilians. Depressing.

Between Saarbrucken and the Rhine River was Hitler's once-mighty West Wall. It was the Siegfried Line, named for the legendary German hero, a knight known as Siegfried. This string of forts was Germany's main defense barrier west of the big river. Hitler began building this in 1936 and it stretched 400 miles from Switzerland to Holland. In places, the line extended more than twenty miles deep. There were thousands of thick concrete pillboxes with interlocking fields of fire. There were also row upon row of appropriately named dragon's teeth, concrete pyramids designed to stop enemy tanks. Hundreds of minefields lay scattered throughout the concrete pillars. The Allies managed to outflank and smash through these formidable fortifications with armored divisions, infantry, and of course the P-47s. Later, each of us in the 50th Fighter Group received the Distinguished Unit Citation for spearheading the attack by the Seventh Army during the assault on the Siegfried Line.

We saw a welcome sight as the convoy rolled up to the first row of dragon's teeth. A freshly painted sign told us that we were entering the Siegfried Line courtesy of a combat engineers outfit from the U.S. Seventh Army. Reassuring to say the least. These concrete obstacles were about six feet high, coming to a point at the top, kind of like small Washington Monuments. I had always pictured these obstacles built in a solid straight line. Not true. They marched in a straight line for maybe a hundred yards and then zigzagged slightly for another hundred yards, and on and on for hundreds of miles. So we just followed a new, improved wide swath through these concrete teeth and finally came out the other side face to face with gigantic empty pillboxes. You

Above, 10th Fighter Squadron convoy moves into Germany at the border town of Saarbrucken. The vehicles drove atop the rubble on a path cleared by the engineers. Below, "dragon's teeth" on Germany's legendary Siegfried Line. The barrier stretched 400 miles from Switzerland to Holland. In places it was more than 20 miles deep.

could see it would have been extremely tough to hammer through this maze without air support.

Next stop for our convoy was the mighty Rhine where we bivouacked overnight on its grassy banks. Nobody was eager to cross at night. Except for the once flourishing cities that lay in smoldering ruins along its banks the Rhine was a magnificent river, maybe a half-mile wide where we camped. Some of the guys slept in their trucks but most of us just picked a soft-looking spot, put a blanket on the ground and one on top, removed our boots and slept in our clothes. Camping under the stars wasn't bad as long as the weather was okay—which it was.

Not far downstream was the high rock cliff where Teutonic legends tell of the beautiful, naked but wicked Lorelei. She lured boatmen to their deaths with her seductive singing while combing her long blond hair. There are countless other stories that make up Germany's national mystique along the Rhine. Composer Richard Wagner added one of his famous operas to a Rhine legend: "The Ring of the Nibelung" in which Rhine maidens controlled a ring made of Rhine gold that gave unlimited power to its wearer.

For twenty centuries the Rhine had been the most formidable barrier to armies attempting to invade German lands. The river was part of Hitler's famous *Festung Europa* (Fortress Europe) but now his fortress was crumbling.

Next morning we ate a K ration breakfast and loaded up for the Rhine crossing. First thing I saw on the riverbank was another sign, this one reading:

> ALEXANDER PATCH BRIDGE
> YOU ARE CROSSING THE RHINE RIVER
> ON THIS PONTOON BRIDGE
> CONSTRUCTED UNDER ARTILLERY FIRE
> BY THE 85th ENGINEERS, 7th U.S. ARMY.

By this time there were dozens of Allied bridges of all kinds spanning the Rhine. The Seventh Army put two infantry divisions across this bridge at Worms (nice name for a town) where we crossed. We waited until 200 German soldiers were herded from the other side before we moved.

This bridge was one of many constructed to get Allied troops across the Rhine barrier. The Germans had methodically blown up all the bridges—except the Ludendorff Bridge at the town of Remagen. Explosives failed to demolish it, so it became a gift to the Americans just reaching the river.

We crossed the Rhine on this pontoon bridge there at Worms, an exciting trip because the bridge swayed and buckled with the current. As we drove off the other side we entered the good-sized town of Worms, still burning and almost obliterated by heavy artillery and fighter-bombers. Turns out that Worms was the town where Martin Luther was officially denounced for attacking the Catholic Church in the sixteenth century. The minute we reached the other side I could see a change in the people and the country-side. It was a lot like Ruidoso, New Mexico, the best looking country I'd seen in Europe. It was difficult to understand why the Germans weren't satisfied with all this awesome beauty yet still wanted *Lebensraum* (living space).

People were really furious at the Americans. As we passed through their towns they just stood and glared at us. But they also seemed amazed and astounded at our heavy equipment. There was a steady stream of men, tanks, gigantic trucks, gasoline tankers and all the other tools of war winding through Germany day and night. The P-47s ranged at will. American and British heavies flew overhead constantly and the Germans watched with their mouths open. I wondered what they must have thought of all this mass of equipment. They seemed to realize they were finally beaten.

In the towns we went through as we got farther into Germany, the people all had white flags of surrender hanging out of windows. Civilians reached out of two and three story timbered buildings hanging bed sheets, pillowcases or anything white. It was a reassuring sight.

19

Deep in the Heartland

WE MOVED ON FARTHER toward the heart of Germany and settled in at the town of Wurzburg. It had a pretty good airfield although it badly needed damage repair. Within a few days our planes were flying fighter sweeps over the Ruhr Valley, the industrial center of Germany. Steel mills, coal mines, munitions factories, aircraft plants and everything needed for the Germans to wage a world war filled this vast chunk of Europe. The Allied armies poured unchallenged across the Rhine and most of the Wehrmacht's strength was lost in the wreckage of the Siegfried Line. We believed the Battle of the Ruhr would seal the final destruction of the German military and the overrunning of German territory.

George Patton's chorus of press relations had the whole world convinced that his Third Army was leading the Allied assault on Festung Deutschland. He was miles away from reality since Alexander Patch's Seventh Army roamed far in front.

Settling down in Wurzburg proved a real experience, much

My home in Wurzburg for a few weeks in April 1945. Although it leaked badly, it was a relief having a roof over our heads. This had recently been a German headquarters and there were lots of framed pictures of Hitler in the undamaged rooms. The town had been drained of any male remotely capable of carrying a gun.

different from what we were used to. We moved into German buildings at the airfield, which meant no more looking up at starry nights and slogging around in French mud. My buddies and I scrambled into a large building that had housed German officers, or at least we assumed so because the debris included Nazi paperwork and nice furniture scattered around. Only one problem—this field and these buildings had been thoroughly crushed by high explosives. Some were in complete ruin, others had no roofs, and a few had only three walls. But we settled in and it wasn't half bad.

We didn't fret about possible booby traps or mines because the Germans pulled out on such short notice, they just wanted to get out alive. For me, to be able to look out a window, even if it had no glass, was almost a thrill. The first night, I inherited a German bed complete with mattress and springs. It was wonderful. Next I found some really nice furniture so the place took on a rather homey look. One guy even had a baby grand piano where he slept. Without windowpanes it got real drafty at night, and it was also darker than hell because this whole part of Germany still had no lights. But no matter how good we had it, there were always things to bitch about. Like my quarters leaked badly since a third of the roof was missing. One day it snowed (April in Germany). Pearce and I leaned back in two overstuffed chairs and laughed heartily as these big soft flakes came tumbling down in the boudoir.

After a few nights in the inky black of Wurzburg I began crawling into my new sack and going to sleep early. It wasn't bad, either. Then we had a pleasant surprise. Two of our guys were trying to get out of these drafty rooms and decided to check out the cellar for better quarters. Nobody had ventured down there yet and it was like finding the Lost Padre Mine. One whole end of the cellar was stacked to the ceiling with cases of champagne—an honest to goodness wine cellar. This rich cache was obviously looted by the Germans before they backed out of France, and now it was all ours. Word got around the squadron within minutes and GIs appeared from all around the area. A guy would come up and ask for a bottle, and my two new cellar dwellers would say, "Hell, take a case of the stuff!" Everybody started popping corks, guzzling out of the bottles, and getting gloriously drunk, which didn't take long because most of them were barely out of their teens and had never tasted French champagne, but then neither had I. This was all high quality stuff, good enough for German officers. They had the best of everything since all they had to do was take it. The plumbing no longer worked, because there was no water for the toilets so these maniacs poured bottles of champagne into the tanks, and then flushed the toilets. It actually worked.

The next thing our cellar dwellers did (God bless them) was discover a wooden box of new German pistols. They were the standard German sidearms, 9mm Walthers. Everybody called them P-38s. Anyway, these guys told Pearce and me about the pistols and we scrambled down to take a look. They were all encased in a gray grease-like gunk known as cosmolene. There was also plenty of ammunition. At first our pals didn't want to give us each a P-38 so what we did was threaten their lives. "Besides," I said, "I outrank you bastards." So they came through in great shape and we had a fine time shooting at targets nailed to pine trees. Originally, the official German Army sidearm was the famous Luger. But these required lots of slow handwork and the factories couldn't keep up with demand. So the Germans mass-produced the P-38. It was not a work of art like the Luger. It even had black plastic handgrips—at least ours did.

Another perk at Wurzburg was our own private movie theater. A one-story building not far from our sleeping quarters had probably been a small warehouse. There was a large hole in the roof; the front part had a dirt floor which we swept clean of debris. But otherwise it was in good shape. Somebody got the brilliant idea of putting benches inside so we could see movies without standing up. We had a projector, and a portable generator made electricity. The army was pretty nice about sending in movies for "the morale of the men." One evening we were all waiting for the film to begin when I scraped my foot on something that felt like metal. Turns out it was metal, in the form of a thousand-pound unexploded bomb. We all cleared out and got three of our ordinance guys to check it. They pronounced it one of ours. It had knocked that hole in the roof and buried itself in the floor. But they told us not to worry because the bomb hadn't been armed. "If it ain't armed it can't go off."

This P-47 brought its pilot back safely from a bombing mission near Wurzburg. In one of the other squadrons a pilot hit a steel pole after strafing a train. This sliced over four feet off one of his wings, but he returned safely.

"Sure," I told these brave comrades. I had recently seen a whole flatbed truck full of unarmed bombs blown to smithereens on a French country road. So we all backed out of the theater like Daffy Duck, and the ordinance team worked all night getting rid of our bomb. These ordinance boys were extremely gutsy. They would dig out land mines and do any other dangerous chore and it never seemed to bother them. They were also crazy.

Meanwhile, the Battle of the Ruhr continued on full throttle. Moving east from the Rhine Allied armies stormed into the industrial heart of Germany. One part of the Ruhr was so densely developed with factories and homes that people could travel its fifty-mile length by streetcar. By this time our P-47s just roamed the skies over the Ruhr searching for targets of opportunity. That is, anything that moved, kill it. In the small villages you seldom saw a church steeple. I always wondered about that until one of the pilots told me the Germans climbed up into these steeples where they had a perfect view of the whole town. Up there snipers picked off American soldiers and did lots of major damage before being detected. Once a sniper was spotted, ground troops radioed the nearest roaming P-47 giving the location of the town and a particular church. This was the kind of ground-air coordination the fighter-bombers were known for. Besides, even in this huge Ruhr Valley, the planes were usually within five minutes away from any action. After receiving his radio coordinates a Thunderbolt pilot would zoom over the treetops about twenty feet above steeple level. With a long burst from all eight .50-caliber machine guns church steeples exploded in flames. Just disappeared.

Most fighter planes had machine guns mounted far apart on the wings. If the guns fired straight ahead, the rounds were likely to scatter all over a fairly large area. The solution was to have all the guns aim at the same small point. This was a relatively simple job for a couple of armorers. You could manually angle the guns inwards and the rounds all converged at the same spot. The impact of hundreds of .50-caliber rounds hitting, say, a ten-foot target was unbelievable.

Some say the expression "the whole nine yards" was invented by British Spitfire fighter pilots. They said the machine gun ammunition belts measured a total of twenty-seven feet. If a pilot fired all his rounds at a target, he would say that it got the whole nine yards. Different aircraft also made completely different sounds. At rooftop level a P-51 fighter plane had a screaming, powerful roar. The much heavier P-47s came over the treetops with a thunderous roar that German troops described as deafening and extremely frightening. The sputtering old Stuka dive-bombers, the terrors of 1940, had a high-pitched whine that was produced by a pair of sirens.

My uncle, Charles Little, served in the North African campaign before leading a Signal Corps outfit in Europe. In Germany enemy snipers killed as many as 50 percent of some of these advance signal units.

Things were looking up for us in Germany, and we were now finding the war strangely tolerable. More of our troops received leaves to Paris. We got cigarettes, the usual carton a week that we had gotten back in Normandy before the supply lines shriveled up. The squadron received another decoration—a second Distinguished Unit Citation for destroying the Luftwaffe's Bad Aibling Aerodrome near Munich. The 50th Group destroyed ninety-eight planes and damaged fifty-seven. They called us all out for the presentation of a little star to pin on the original blue and gold ribbons. The Belgian Army also cited us in the Order of the Day. The only reason I could think of was that we helped kick the Nazi's butts out of Belgium as well as getting rid of the French people's blight.

The Battle of the Ruhr ended when American armored divisions formed a giant pincer encircling nearly all of the German troops in the Ruhr Valley. Its once-flourishing industrial cities lay in ruins created in part by the savage Allied aerial assault. The Allies captured 325,000 German prisoners in the Ruhr. The end of the war was in sight.

20

The Fall of the Third Reich

IT WAS APRIL 1945. Allied armies closed in on the Germans from all directions. Their cities lay in ruins, still burning. Their armies and divisions had lost communications with each other. Their generals knew that it was long past time to surrender. But Hitler ordered them to keep fighting to the last man, and as a result thousands of both German and Allied troops died tragically for no reason except Hitler's lunacy. The Luftwaffe was grounded for lack of aviation fuel and new pilots. Constant bombing by the RAF and the American Eighth and Ninth Air Forces pulverized Hitler's dwindling territory on an unendurable scale.

In Wurzburg we knew the war couldn't last more than a few weeks. But we began to hear rumors of a "National Redoubt." Supposedly, the Nazi intention was to skim off the finest of the SS, Gestapo, and other fanatical German troops and send them into the mountains of Bavaria, Austria, and northern Italy. There they would block high passes in the Alps and hold out indefinitely in a drawn-out type of guerilla warfare. This sounds like an impossible dream now, but in 1945 it seemed clear that Germany intended to do just that.

Eisenhower and his Supreme Headquarters staff assumed the redoubt could be the scene of a desperate stand by the remaining German armies. And these were still impressive. They totaled about 100 partial infantry divisions, most of the remaining armored and SS formations and up to 30 panzer divisions. The plan was that these would be concentrated behind the mountain barriers, with Berchtesgaden as the seat of government. In addition, most of the German jet fighter plane strength was already located in the south.

We had been planning all along to eventually get to Berlin and it was disappointing to find out that was not in Eisenhower's plans. The Russians were already only thirty miles from Berlin and would get there long before we could. Also, to capture a city that had lost all its military and political clout, the resulting heavy loss of American lives would be stupid. So Berlin was out. Since then I have always felt lucky that we didn't get there.

American troops all over the world were saddened to learn about President Roosevelt's death on April 12, only weeks before Germany's collapse. The Third Reich lay in ruins. On April 30 Hitler married his mistress Eva Braun and they committed suicide in his Berlin bunker. Two days later Berlin fell to the invading Russian armies. On May 4 the American Seventh Army, which we were with, received orders to cease-fire. At the same time our squadron got the order to "stand down." Early on the morning of May 7 German General Alfred Jodl entered a red school building in Reims, France and signed the terms of Germany's unconditional surrender.

The same morning, our commanding officer sent for me regarding an address to the troops about an "important event." He asked me to stand by with my Speed Graphic so that I could capture the reaction after his announcement. Word passed

American planes dropped these safe conduct leaflets over enemy troops in the spring of 1945. Realizing the war was lost, German troops surrendered by the thousands.

quickly to the squadron, and for the benefit of those who were out of hearing distance, the commanding officer also notified our bugler (yes we actually had a bugler who didn't get to play very often) to play Assembly so all would be present and accounted for. I can't recall his name but everybody called him the Little Guinea (political correctness didn't exist then). He was an Italian kid from Brooklyn. I wondered why so many Italian kids were always from Brooklyn. Anyway he was darn good. As soon as everybody assembled, the C.O. read Eisenhower's "Victory Order of the Day," announcing that the war in Europe was finally over. Nobody moved or clapped or shouted. I'm hunched down with my Speed Graphic, set on f-16 at a 100th waiting to capture the victory celebration. Nothing happened, not a word. They just stood there. It was kind of eerie but I knew down deep what those guys were feeling and thinking. They were all just drained mentally and physically. And at that moment nothing needed to be said.

Even though there was no wild celebration on V-E-Day, we all breathed a sigh of relief that it was Over Over There. Of course, the usual rumors began within hours. On the day of the surrender three million Americans were under Eisenhower's command, including sixty-one full divisions. The first rumor from the mill was that the 50th Fighter Group would move as quickly as possible to Marseilles and then ship out direct to the Pacific. The next rumor had us going back to a staging area at Reims and from there to the States for thirty-day furloughs before heading to the Pacific. Then we heard very authoritatively that we could remain in Germany as part of the occupation force. We all liked rumor No. 2 and hated the others. All I wanted was to get the hell out of there and go home. We were all really anxious to get back even if it meant heading out again—for Japan. Most of us felt realistically that we'd never make it back after Japan, a negative feeling but I felt that the Japs would be bloody murder.

This was the Salzburg airdrome where mint condition German planes sat idle because of a lack of fuel and pilots. This plane, however, was riddled by several hundred bullet holes.

At least most Germans would put their hands on top of their heads and surrender. I heard any number of times that Japanese women and kids would fight with sharpened bamboo spears right on the beaches. That's not exactly what I had in mind.

Anyway, some but not all of us would be moving around again within the next several days. Our executive officer announced that a small convoy from the 10th was going down to Bavaria and take a look at Hitler's controversial National Redoubt and the big Luftwaffe airfield at Salzburg, Austria. I usually followed the army's hard and fast philosophy, "never volunteer." But this time I broke the rule again and signed up. Besides I was sick of our airfield at Wurzburg. It turned out to be a good decision.

Next morning about twenty of us in two trucks and two jeeps, led by a lieutenant and a captain, left Wurzburg and headed for

Nuremberg, the heart of Nazi country. The backs of the jeeps were unbelievably crowded. Each carried extra five-gallon gas cans (they're still called Jerry cans), five-gallon water cans, carbines, ammunition, maps, sleeping bags and boxes of what were called 10-in-1 rations. The trucks carried more of the same, in addition to us.

Near dusk we pulled into Nuremberg, a town that was to become famous for the Nuremberg War Criminal Trials. It was a walled, moated place that Hitler called the most German of all German cities. Now the once-lovely town sprawled almost completely destroyed. There was lots of debris in the streets but we drove through without any major problems with the locals. They had the usual white sheets and surrender flags hanging out of upstairs windows. They also met us with silence and sullen, hostile stares. It didn't bother us since we weren't exactly Miss Congeniality ourselves.

Our captain had an up-to-date map and he pointed us toward a huge stadium near the center of the city. This was the stadium you still see in film documentaries, with Hitler atop the magnificent podium proclaiming the Thousand Year Reich. These were nighttime party rallies where thousands of Nazi troops in full regalia carried torches and marched to military music. Hundreds of flagpoles flew huge red banners with white circles in the center containing large black swastikas. It was easy to visualize how these magical torchlight events influenced the German people to blindly follow der Fuehrer. These were the same people who were telling us they weren't really Nazis. Above the main podium a giant gold swastika surrounded by gold leaves twenty feet high had only recently looked down on the crowds. The first American troops to enter the stadium expertly blew this symbol into small pieces.

When we pulled into the stadium we noticed the field was occupied by part of an American armored division that had captured the city. Nuremberg, on Hitler's personal orders, fought to the bitter end. American Sherman tanks were everywhere, their crews sitting around eating supper. We stopped for a moment and then these guys invited us to "come on in, there's room for everybody." I've always wondered if they were the ones who blew away that big swastika. I should have asked. Next morning I ate a big juicy K ration for breakfast, sitting right on top of the podium where Hitler used to stand and captivate the multitudes. After breakfast I took pictures of my buddies one at a time, standing up on the podium with one arm raised in the Nazi salute and the other holding a pocket comb on their upper lip. Everybody got their pictures taken but me—the photographer. C'est la guerre.

21

Dachau

AFTER SPENDING THE NIGHT around a campfire in the Nuremberg Stadium we stowed our gear and headed for Munich. Before leaving, the captain called us unto a huddle for instructions. There will be no fraternization with German civilians. Don't whistle at pretty girls. Do travel in threes and stay well armed. These people are mad as hell, so don't mess with them. We will spend every night in their houses. Knock on the door, then give them ten minutes to take their belongings and get out. The magic word is *Raus* and they understand that. They also understand that if they are on the street after dark they will be shot. We may go through a town that has surrendered but remaining German soldiers aren't aware of that. They know the war is over, but don't count on it. Especially, don't do anything stupid. End of speech.

We wound our way through the rubble of Nuremberg and headed due south toward Munich and the Bavarian Alps. Fortunately, one of our guys, a sergeant named Hilmar Haas, spoke fluent German. He was a Texan from the Hill Country near

Fredericksburg. Everybody just called him Hoss. He was well over six feet tall, blond, and looked like Germans were supposed to look. We pulled into Munich later in the day and found a nice, unburned neighborhood that looked okay to spend the night. Hoss went with the rest of us as we banged on doors to advise the locals that they had an hour to vacate before we moved in. Most of the houses were middle class two story affairs, just about right for four or five of us. I entered a house in which the residents were an elderly man and his wife, a teenage girl and a guy about thirty who was a dead ringer for an SS officer. He was wearing leather shorts, which in Bavaria are called *lederhosen*. He had a bullet-like shaved head and could have passed for a young Eric von Stroheim. Call Central Casting. I was certain he had very recently walked away from the Wehrmacht, but all I was interested in was one of his soft beds. These people had a small guesthouse in the back yard, so they took some of their possessions and moved there. They showed little emotion. They were dumbfounded.

It's worth mentioning here that as conquerors, most American soldiers were pretty decent. GIs weren't supposed to take private property, but generally they took what they wanted. And that didn't include some old girl's wedding china and silverware. They didn't rape, loot, pillage, and burn their way through Germany. Most GIs (they called it liberating) just wanted some wartime souvenirs. And I was no different. I liberated a couple of Nazi dress daggers and several swastika armbands from our gracious hosts in Munich, who swore they were not Nazis and didn't know anything about the festering death camp at Dachau, only twenty miles away.

In Germany, Munich is called Munchen. I remember one morning while still in France I asked my fighter pilot friend George Johnson, who was about to take off, where he was headed that morning. He smiled and answered, "Luncheon in Munchen."

My memory gets a bit fuzzy over the years but for some crazy reason I still remember those immortal words.

Munich was the cradle of the Nazi Party, the scene of Hitler's renowned Beer Hall Putsch in 1923. It was here in Munich, the capital of Bavaria, that Hitler and his gang of cutthroats would attract over a million people to such events as a harvest festival or party rally to hear him speak. In Nuremberg, that stadium seated 125,000 ecstatic Germans raising their arms in the Nazi salute while watching the magical nighttime spectacles. Thousands of uniformed, black booted and helmeted troops carried torches and marched to the national anthem and military drumbeats. PR at its frenzied best.

We pulled out of Munich early in the morning and headed south to the town of Dachau. The huge concentration camp was nearby, and the civilians just shrugged and gave you that palms up "who me" look when you asked about the nearby "murder school" for members of the SS. They didn't know anything about it. But the camp had only been in their neighborhood since 1933. Give us a break. Heinrich Himmler established it and it became the model for Germany's concentration camps. Dachau was un-like any terror system ever devised. Freight cars arrived almost daily and unloaded their cargoes of humanity. Men were usually separated from women and children. The men were made to disrobe and stand naked, packed together for twenty-four hours. Many died, many could stand only a few hours and as soon as they slumped to the ground they were shot and killed on the spot. The others worked as slave labor in local German armament factories in Dachau until they died of malnutrition or disease carried by rats. Their usefulness lasted only a few months but that was no problem since new prisoners filled their ranks. Meanwhile, newly arriving women and children were executed by SS rifles and bulldozed into common graves. All you've heard or seen of these camps is true. One old girl, the wife of an SS man, made lampshades out of the tattooed skin of prisoners.

Most of the SS abandoned the camp the same week Germany surrendered in 1945, not a moment too soon. I think American infantrymen who liberated more than 67,000 Dachau prisoners would have executed the SS guards right there. Meanwhile, the SS hurriedly evacuated other concentration camps and moved the prisoners to different locations. These relocations took about a week, usually walking. Thousands of prisoners died on the way because of sickness, weakness, starvation or beatings by the SS. When they could no longer walk the guards shot them. The day our convoy drove through the wide-open gates, an American major walked over and asked if we could give him and the other troops a hand in getting the prisoners out of this god-awful horror as quickly as possible. Our captain's answer was "That's what we're here for."

We piled out of the trucks and began helping other GIs load prisoners into army vehicles. These prisoners were all men. I never saw any women or children. Many of these pitiful looking men were dying right in front of us. They nearly all wore vertically striped black and gray pajama-like outfits. Many were naked, literally skin and bones. Those who were able were so grateful they tried to embrace us but the major who was running this operation told me not to let them touch us because so many of them had typhus and other diseases. So you just had to smile and lift them into trucks. Since the prisoners' barracks were hopelessly overcrowded with "bunks" six and seven layers deep, and with dying or dead prisoners lying on floors in their own human waste, typhus epidemics took thousands of lives. The smell of death permeated everything, even our clothes. I know you've heard much of this before, but it bears repeating.

Dachau prided itself on its so-called medical and scientific experiments using live prisoners as guinea pigs. One such experiment was to immerse a prisoner in a tub of ice water to find out exactly how long it took him to die. Some were forced to exist on seawater to find out how long a human could survive at sea without food or fresh water.

Polish Jews were the largest national group sent to Dachau, but ultimately prisoners from more than thirty countries met their fate there. As early as 1938, during the infamous *Kristallnacht* (Crystal Night) truckloads of young Nazis smashed the glass windows of hundreds of stores in Berlin's Jewish ghetto. Then they brought 10,000 Jews into Dachau to die.

No doubt about it, the Nazis were bent on genocide, the elimination of an entire people. This whole place was unreal. The sickly sweet, nauseating smell of death assailed all your senses. You had to experience it to believe it. You've heard about man's inhumanity to man; this should go down in history as the place where it was invented. It's difficult to put it into words, but Dachau and many others like it, wasn't just a venue to kill people and bury them. The Nazis methodically dehumanized them first by using any number of cruelties, like stripping them naked outside in the middle of winter, forcing young mothers to watch their babies bashed to death. Women and girls were routinely raped. Sadistic guards hung people on meat hooks like sides of beef and tormented them with laughter while they cut out their intestines so the prisoners could watch them drag on the floor. I don't know if there was ever in history an era in which humans behaved quite like this. The Romans had their Coliseum and gladiators, the Turks exterminated nearly all the Armenians in the twentieth century, and other civilizations tried to outdo each other in killing and maiming but for sheer dehumanizing, bizarre cruelty, I can't think of any one group that was as rotten as the Nazis in World War II.

22

Berchtesgaden

WITH RELIEF WE GOT BACK in our convoy, away from the awful stench in Dachau and away from Munich where all this first started. After another night as guests of our Munich hosts the captain wanted to get going early, with no breakfast. Nobody argued. There would always be a decent spot to stop on the side of the road. We convoyed down the autobahn between Munich and Salzburg, heading for Berchtesgaden. Admittedly, the autobahn was a classy highway, especially since few of us had ever seen anything like it in America. The nearest thing to it that I'd seen was in 1940. It was called the Pasadena Speedway in Los Angeles. As we tooled along, we began to see great looking airplanes parked near the side of the autobahn, partially hidden by the pine forest. No propellers. They had to be the first jets any of us had seen, the Messerschmitt-262 jet fighter. One was parked fairly near the road, so the captain decided this was a good place to pull over, check out this airplane, and eat lunch.

Most of our food supplies were pretty good—a long way from

our usual Cs. These were the 10-in-1s, meaning each wax-covered carton held enough to feed ten men for one day or one man for ten days. Somebody's thinking back there in Washington. The menu varied from carton to carton. Each one contained two pounds of thick sliced bacon (which you could fry in your mess kit). There were large size no-melt chocolate bars and, of course, the usual cans of cheese and crackers and coffee and lemonade and all the rest. In addition to the olive drab toilet paper there was always a carton of cigarettes. Jesus, where do you go to reenlist?

Unfortunately for the Wehrmacht, the Me-262 jets didn't arrive in any quantity until late in the war. The RAF and American heavies had devastated German aircraft factories in the Ruhr Valley so that production of the new fighter slowed to a trickle. Allied raids of 1,000 planes were commonplace. Replacements for downed German fighter pilots were almost nonexistent. And the lack of fuel, due to Allied bombing of refineries and huge oil fields like Ploesti in Rumania, finally grounded the jets. That was the last straw—out of gas for the duration. That was the predicament the jets were in when we saw them sitting near the autobahn on our way to Berchtesgaden. Since all of us were airplane freaks, we delighted in just looking and touching these machines. They could fly 540 miles an hour, much faster than our fighters and they succeeded in shooting down several hundred Allied planes before being grounded. In appearance, they resembled a cross between an RAF Spitfire and an American P-51 —only more streamlined.

On the road again we climbed into the snow-capped peaks of the Bavarian Alps. So far this part of Germany seemed relatively unscathed by the war. It wasn't anything like the Germany we'd just left. The little villages were something you'd see in a picture book—or Disneyland. Lots of A-frame houses with flower boxes in the windows and white cattle with tinkling bells hanging around their necks. The people didn't seem angry like those we had passed farther north where battle damage was everywhere. We drove down the narrow cobblestone streets through the towns and noticed that nobody had bothered to drape white surrender flags from second story windows. Julie Andrews would have been right at home in these hills.

The girls wore colorful full skirts with dirndls over starched white puffy blouses. They all dressed pretty much alike and their hairstyles were similar—long braided hair (lots of blonds) that hung down the front of their blouses. For once, everything looked like I thought it should. Except that we saw very few men and boys. I guess they were back in France still trying to kill us. I remembered seeing the personal effects of dead German soldiers and they invariably had photos in their wallets of happy family groups smiling for some special occasion. Their pets were there too, all posing in front of their gardens. Happy, healthy, freshly scrubbed, handsome people. I got to wondering, "what's wrong with this picture?" Under any circumstances, how could people who looked like this, who had dogs and cats and lived in splendid Alpine homes surrounded by flowers be a part of what we had just seen in Dachau? How could this fairytale land have produced some of the most evil men in history?

I thought a lot about that question—and still do. I've yet to come up with an answer. In some German houses the people we kicked out would point to themselves and say "No Nazi, no Nazi," Then later we'd see family snapshots with the whole family dressed up with all the Nazi stuff—the full regalia. They told us they were forced to join up, but when Hitler was riding high and killing millions of unfortunate people these same civilians were all out in the streets and stadiums watching torchlight parades and heiling their heads off.

We finally pulled off the autobahn near the Austrian border, and here was our destination, Berchtesgaden, a storybook village if there ever was one. Most of the buildings were two and

This guy told me his name was Hans—and I still believe it. He wore the perfect combination of Tyrolean garb, from the feather in his cap to his leather pants. He was scavenging lumber from the ruins of Berchtesgaden and didn't seem to hate the GIs. I figured he was happy to see the top Nazis forced out.

three story and seemed to be all different colors. Until then I had a negative, black feeling about this place, but it was obvious that I associated it with Hitler's symbolic home and the worst of the Nazis. Even the name Berchtesgaden held an ominous feeling for me. Located near the top of a peak was Hitler's secret retreat, called the Berghof. It was here, some 2,000 feet above Berchtesgaden, that Europe's top leaders came to be counseled (and humiliated) during the late 1930s. In addition to Hitler's impressive home and huge meeting room, were the personal homes away from home for his highest-ranking leadership— Himmler, Goebbels, Borman, Goering and others. There were

A sketch of der Fuhrer I made on a letter sent home. Hitler was easy to draw since his picture hung in half the buildings we entered.

apartments and barracks for SS troops who held tight security around the entire mountain, patrolling day and night. Eva Braun, Hitler's pretty blond live-in girlfriend, could always be counted on to enliven festivities and banquets at the Berghof.

This place had been a veritable treasure trove, with loot from all over Europe stashed by the top Nazis. Art treasures like paintings by Rembrandt and all of the French impressionists, as well as jewelry and millions of dollars in currency were in this huge estate overlooking Berchtesgaden. Rumors and intelligence reports continued to surface about Nazi plans to establish their National Redoubt after the official end of the war and that Berchtesgaden would be the capital. To help stifle that plan, the American Eighth Air Force thoroughly pounded this stronghold and symbol of Nazi arrogance, leaving much of the Berghof a smoking ruin. Even so, it contained the best looting possibilities in Europe. Everybody was trying to get there first; the French, the British, Germans who wanted to retrieve their possessions and every American in Germany. The famous 101st Airborne and the 3rd Infantry Division got there first. Some of

Hitler's secret retreat, the Berghof, as it looked after a pounding by the American Eighth Air Force. It was here, 2,000 feet above the town of Berchtesgaden, that Europe's top leaders came to be counseled and humiliated during the late 1930s. This had been a veritable treasure trove, with loot from all over Europe stashed by the top Nazis.

the paratroopers were already driving black Mercedes by the time we arrived.

Although most of the wonderful goodies were already liberated, I did spy a number of fancy wall sconces that had been used to light up Hitler's main room. Since they were such prosaic and civilized looking pieces, nobody seemed to notice them—or they figured they were kind of sissy. I quickly decided that ol' Mangan didn't come all the way across the Atlantic Ocean and half the countries in Europe to go home empty handed. So I tried to pry one off the wall. It wouldn't budge. You've got to hand it to the Germans, when they build something it's there forever. Anyway, I got another kid to help me pry, and after much groaning and swearing it came out of the wall. However, on the way out one of it's sharp edges cut a nasty gash in the palm of my right hand. But I didn't even scream for a medic because by that time they were saying, "Hey look at them neat light fixtures!" Now everybody wanted one of Hitler's personal belongings. Best of luck you bastards. In a couple of weeks my hand healed up and I'm happy to say that was my most serious (if not heroic) war wound.

I hauled that lamp half way around the Free World, finally found a large carton and sent it to my mother in El Paso. I'm also happy to report that this same lighting sconce hangs on my office wall to this day, still shining brightly. The best thing Hitler had in his front room was this huge picture window where he and his party drones could relax and enjoy one of the greatest views of all time. This heavy plate glass was about twenty feet wide and six feet high. The Austrian Tyrol spread out below with gingerbread homes spotted around on the lush green rolling pastures backed up by snow capped Alpine mountains. What a setting for *The Sound of Music.* I always figured that American architects and builders picked up on Hitler's window design and put thousands of them in new homes after the war. Problem was if you looked out your new picture window the chances were you would be looking at your neighbor looking at you through his window across the street.

23

All Quiet on the Western Front

We pulled out of Berchtesgaden and headed for Austria. Salzburg to be exact. Fading rumors still floated around that the Salzburg Airport was intact and legions of Nazi fanatics planned to use this as a base for guerilla warfare in the mountains of southern Bavaria, western Austria, and northern Italy. About half way to Salzburg we rolled into a little town, and sure enough it was crawling with German soldiers, armed and I assumed dangerous. (A year earlier when we were moving from place to place so often, we joked that one of these days we'd enter a town only to find that nobody had informed the Germans, who had an attitude about Americans anyway.)

We drove slowly up Main Strasse and sitting on the steps of what looked like a courthouse was this German officer calmly getting his boots shined by a small boy. He wore a sidearm but seemed unconcerned that the American army was invading his town. He looked splendid in his dress uniform. Then we all gawked at another officer on the sidewalk waiting to cross the

*Even while retreating, the Germans took time to welcome us with signs
like this.*

cobblestone street. He stood stiffly erect like Nazi officers in
Hollywood movies. He also carried a Luger. Like the other chap,
he didn't order us to surrender and was not concerned that we
outnumbered him and his pal about twenty to one. Then as we
crossed a little side street I could see in the next block what looked
like an entire German infantry regiment.

These guys were sitting outside their pup tents. They placed
their rifles close by, about eight guns to a pyramidal stack much
like we used to do in high school ROTC. This whole scene was
more than a bit unsettling, and I hoped that my companions
remembered the immortal words of our wise captain "Don't do
anything stupid." We just plowed slowly through town looking
over our shoulders at that sea of gray uniforms in the pasture.
It became obvious that all these soldiers and their officers
surrendered to some American unit that didn't know what to
do with them. The Americans probably told them to stack their
arms and sit tight. At this point they knew the war was over—

as we did. And who in their right mind wanted to get killed after the war is over?

It was an easy truck ride from Berchtesgaden in Germany to Salzburg in Austria. But the Austrians were light years ahead in their feelings toward the American army. In some towns the people actually smiled and waved at us. Little kids ran up to our trucks and wanted a ride. They also asked for gum and candy, even Lifesavers. But little kids are the same no matter where you go. They are fun loving and brave, and not old enough to hate us like the legendary Hitler Youth who were teenagers. I could feel the relief the Austrians showed after the Germans evacuated. The Germans took a few written pot shots at us with paintbrushes as they moved out. Even while retreating, they took the time to paint messages for us on the sides of barns. I remember one that was painted in white on a big dark gray barn. Letters three feet high read:

DIE FOR AMERICA
AND SAVE THE TOMMY

In spite of the unwelcome Nazi propaganda, the scenery as we neared Salzburg was some of the best I'd seen. Dense fir forests climbed up to the snow line on the Alpine peaks. Clear mountain streams tumbled down the valleys. In short, it was breathtaking. I pointed this out to my comrades in arms but they were singularly unimpressed. One thing they couldn't help but notice, though, was the complete absence of billboards along the highways. Not even Burma Shave signs. Julie Andrews where were you?

Salzburg was in pretty good shape. American MPs waved us into the Salzburg Airport, and stretching as far as we could see were German military planes. The field was captured intact; consequently the aircraft were in mint condition. There were a few jet fighters, and lots of Messerschmitt 109s and Focke-Wulf 190s.

Even Hermann Goering's private plane was parked there looking lost. It was a three-engine Fokker, a little smaller than
America's DC-3. I never saw so many swastikas and black crosses
in my life, and it gave us a nice warm feeling to know these planes
weren't going anywhere because they had run out of gas. We
walked around and looked at the fighters, the same kind that had
been trying to maim us at our forward landing strips.

Then we headed for Innsbruck and the Brenner Pass into Italy.
It was less than a hundred miles to Innsbruck and we made it
easily before dark, even with these big old trucks groaning up
and down mountain roads. We picked out a decent neighborhood
and began our usual knock on the doors to greet the neighbors
and tell them to evacuate. I still found it difficult to tell some
hausfrau she's got an hour to haul out the family belongings. But
that was the official U.S. policy and the army really didn't want
you feeling sorry for these people. Don't even speak to them
after your first "Raus."

In all the towns that were open, military government had
posted big bulletins with regulations printed in German and
English. But I always felt like Simon Legree brandishing the
mortgage when I saw little girls bawling and dragging away
their limp dolls and stuff. It really was pitiful, but what are you
going to do?

Next day we parked alongside the Inn River for a breakfast of
10-in-1 bacon. Some Germans civilians stood on the riverbank
trout fishing, and I know the aroma of bacon frying in our mess
kits drove them nuts. It even drove me nuts. After breakfast one
of the Germans could see that I was intently watching him handle
that fly rod. He held it out toward me and asked in German if I
wanted to try my luck. I flicked a leader into that churning mass
of cold water. Naturally I didn't catch anything, but I hadn't seen
that much water since the Rhine and it was fun for a few minutes. That no-fraternization policy wasn't working.

Hermann Goering's private plane sits among dozens of Luftwaffe aircraft at the Salzburg airport. The field was captured intact, so the military aircraft were all flyable. It was a warm feeling to get a close look at the planes that had been bugging us since Normandy.

We crossed the river on a steel bridge the army engineers had just completed. They put up a small sign reading ERNIE PYLE MEMORIAL BRIDGE. Pyle was America's most read and revered war correspondent and it did my heart good to see that sign in Austria. From Innsbruck it was only a short ride, due south to Brenner Pass and the Italian border.

Is it just me or do you think the Germans had a knack for naming things with strong, even fearsome connotations? The words Brenner Pass seemed a bit foreboding and dangerous. America would have named it Bluebonnet Pass. The Germans used a skull and crossbones and lightning bolts on their SS black uniforms. The American 69th Division called itself the Rainbow Division and their uniform shoulder patch was a full color rainbow. Is that going to scare an enemy? The Germans had panzer divisions, the Luftwaffe, Tiger tanks. We had the Air Corps, armored divisions with Sherman tanks. Even our own esteemed

10th Fighter Squadron logo was The Peashooters.

Some of us walked across Brenner Pass so we could write the folks back home that we had been to Italy. The infantry troops here were all Fifth Army soldiers who had come up the hard way through Italy. When I turned around to head back the first thing I noticed was a professional looking sign that read:

> You are now entering
> AUSTRIA
> thru the courtesy
> of the
> 6th U.S. CORPS
> Salerno Volturno Anzio Rome
> S. France Alsace Danube Germany

It was obvious there would be no National Redoubt. The roads were lined with thousands of people, all walking. These were newly freed slave laborers, Poles, Russians, French, Italians, people from every country in Europe. Whole families, kids, old ladies with heavy packs on their backs going God knows where, heading for home wherever that was. Thousands of them were German civilians who had no place to go. They were especially cautious since the Fatherland had just lost a six-year popularity contest. The other civilians hated their guts. Lots of people smiled and waved at us even though they were tragic, homeless victims. Up there on Austria's southern border you would see thousands of Italians heading home in groups of maybe three or four. One guy would be pulling a little kid's wagon loaded with junk. Somebody's mama would be pushing a broken-down baby carriage full of her earthly belongings, with a big red, white and green Italian flag flapping in the breeze.

It was hard to realize that these people were walking right over the top of the Alps, through Brenner Pass, down into Italy and pulling a damn waggon all the way. And it was the same all

American troops loved to paint signs telling you they got there first. This one was in Italy on the Austrian border at Brenner Pass.

over. Frenchmen were walking from Berlin to Paris, and that's another long walk. These people were all DPs. Since there was yet no means of transporting millions of people back to their homes the Allies set up massive DP camps. Thousands of Poles and Russians were still prisoners in a sense because of the distances. We were not allowed to talk to them. Why, I didn't know. But we talked to them anyway. Go ahead, draft me.

THE STARS AND STRIPES

GERMANY EDITION
Volume 1, No. 34
Tuesday, May 8, 1945

Daily Newspaper of U.S. Armed Forces   on the European Theater of Operations

EXTRA

NAZIS QUIT!

Doenitz Gives Order

Unconditional surrender of all German forces was announced yesterday by the German radio at Flensburg.

Grand Adm. Doenitz, successor to Hitler, ordered the surrender and the German High Command declared it effective, the German announcement said.

There was no immediate announcement from the capitals of the Allied powers, but Associated Press and Reuter correspondents assigned to SHAEF stated unofficially that the Germans had surrendered unconditionally to the western Allies and Russia at 0241 Monday (ETO time).

High German officers formally surrendered the German forces at a meeting in the big red schoolhouse which is Gen. Eisenhower's headquarters, the AP and Reuter reported.

Although there was no Allied announcement, the British Ministry of Information said that today (Tuesday) would be considered as V-E Day.

Not waiting for formal confirmation of the peace news, New York and battered London, beflagged as never before, began celebrations.

(Continued on Page 4)

24

It's Over Over There

IT WAS MID-MAY 1945, shortly after Germany's top remaining generals signed the unconditional surrender in Reims, France. To Eisenhower "unconditional" meant just that. All of the German forces on the Eastern Front wanted to surrender to the Allies, not to the Russians, who were infamous for their brutality toward prisoners of war. German generals knew that thousands of troops would never see their homes again unless they could surrender to the Americans and their allies. So the Germans requested a special condition that would allow the POWs to move into Allied territory. But Eisenhower was adamant that there be no conditions attached to this surrender. And that's the way it went down. As the English used to say quaintly, "It's the war, you know."

The 10th Fighter Squadron's Bavarian convoy made it all the way to Italy without starting World War III and was winding northward through Germany on the way back to Wurzburg. Not much had happened in our absence except more rumors about our future. One improvement occurred, however, and that was our living quarters. The U.S. Army had sanctioned the use of German homes as quarters for American troops. The squadron moved from the piles of debris at the Wurzburg airfield to civilian houses nearby. I knocked on a likely looking door and a German lady answered. She was already acquainted with our housing rules. She knew we weren't from Welcome Wagon.

She began gathering up belongings so we could move in. The next thing that happened was almost unbelievable. An American MP walked up with a young kid in tow. It turned out this kid was a fifteen-year-old German soldier and he was crying, tears streaking down his muddy face. One of those ankle-length overcoats covered his dirty Wehrmacht uniform. The lady I was talking to shrieked with joy and ran down the steps to welcome this apparition. He was her fifteen-year-old son, being escorted home by an American twice his size. You never saw such a happy, tearful homecoming. The lady lost her husband during the war, and this was her only son. She asked me if she could take him upstairs, put him in the bathtub, and give him some fresh, clean clothes. I told her sure and headed to the house next door where we would spend the remaining feather bed nights of our stay in Wurzburg. There I liberated a German beer mug that was inscribed HAUPTBAHNHOFF WURZBURG. This sounded romantic to me until I got home and found out the inscription means Wurzburg Railroad Station. Not overly exciting, but that mug still sits on my bookshelves.

Somewhere along the line I picked up an ugly skin disease. Three weeks without a helmet bath and I was covered from head to foot with a million red itchy sores. I couldn't tell what it was, but some of my acquaintances also had the same thing and they were calling it everything from Chinese rot, seven-year itch, creeping crud, mechanized dandruff, or even worse, crotch crickets. I went to see Captain Cremona, our squadron doctor and he

I took this picture in Mannheim, Germany shortly after the war ended in Europe. The scene seemed to say, "There's been some changes made." This was the first American flag I'd seen for more than a year. I never expected to see a flag bearer and a little drummer boy leading the troops, but that red, white and blue banner was conspicuously absent except in Paris. I was so taken with this image that I sent the photo to LIFE magazine. They took their time sending me a reject slip.

told me it was just a fungus or something caused by being filthy. I thanked him for sharing that with me. He told me to get a bath and a shave and a haircut and new clothes and that should do the trick. I remember hoping it would clear up soon in case I ever got home on furlough. I sure didn't want to show up looking like that.

Since it really was Over Over There life quickly gained momentum. As we had done lots of times before, we loaded up, said farewell to our relatively comfortable quarters, and headed for Mannheim, back on the Rhine River. We were finally headed toward civilization. Yea.

In some parts of Mannheim, like the downtown section, there was nothing left but a mass of ruins. But as in other places, the Americans came in with bulldozers and cut streets right through the debris. This place must have been another one of your picture book German towns, but it was an awful mess when we got there. I figured maybe they could rebuild it some year. The 10th lucked out with living quarters. We moved into really nice stucco houses that all looked alike about two blocks from the Mannheim airport. This neighborhood had fortunately been spared the killer bombing and shelling. We moved into this bunch of two-story homes, taking over the whole area. Eight guys and I lived in a house by ourselves. We had hot and cold running water, electricity, a flush toilet that actually flushed, good feather beds, a kitchen, and a baby grand piano. There was beautiful china and cut glass stuff on the shelves, and bookcases full of Nazi propaganda. We picked up some of the dishes, looked them over, and then put them all back. Who in their right mind wanted somebody's dishes for a war souvenir? Not unlike my feelings back in Wurzburg, this Mannheim was great—sitting in a nice easy chair, looking out a glass window, and knowing that when it rained your blankets weren't going to get sopping wet. This was Sunday on the farm.

As you might surmise, there wasn't much flying anymore, only patrols and fancy formation flying. Time began to hang heavily so naturally the Army hated to see us sitting around. Bad for troop morale. So they began figuring out means to keep the boys busy while sweating out the Pacific Theater. The brass decided we should have calisthenics and sports, especially since they thought we were rapidly getting soft. Actually it worked out pretty well for me. The deal was that if you played sports you didn't have to do calisthenics. Before all this insane activity actually began, a group of my buddies and I wandered into a bunch of shops fairly close to the airfield. The civilians hadn't come back yet, so we poked around in the ruins, just checking things out. One of the gutted buildings had been a sporting goods store, and what was left of the merchandise was still there. Aha, liberation time. The first thing I spotted was a beautiful bamboo vaulting pole and it was already wrapped with white tape. Not only was it undamaged but also the standards and bamboo bar were lying under some plaster and bricks, saying "Take me to your airfield." And besides, it would keep me from doing a thousand side straddle hops.

Back at the base some of us set up a vaulting pit and runway. We used mattress sacks filled with straw (that's where the expression "hit the sack" came from) for a sand pit and had a lot of fun trying to kill ourselves. The other guys played softball and volleyball. We were happy and the officers were happy as they directed our efforts to keep the troops from getting soft. Several of my associates got passes to go to nearby Trossingen in the Black Forest. They came back with all sorts of souvenirs—cuckoo clocks, harmonicas, and one beautiful accordion. They discovered that the Hohner harmonica factory was Trossingen's major industry. The plant was badly bomb-damaged, so these guys just went inside and liberated what they could carry. I got one of the chromatic harmonicas by trading a Nazi armband for it. Hohner was always the Rolls Royce of harmonicas. The one I lost in the Normandy bombing was also a Hohner so I figured somebody—either the Germans or the Allies—owed me a harmonica. I still own it, and play it once in a while.

Soon after our bitching about calisthenics died down, we were treated to what was known as Ground School—two or three hours every morning of training film and lectures. We hated it of course, especially the subjects like Avoiding Venereal Diseases, Malaria: its Cause and Treatment, Living in the Jungle, Mine Laying,

The head office insisted that the troops do calisthenics or sports to keep from getting flabby after VE-Day. I hated the thought of deep knee bends. We liberated a beautiful vaulting pole from a Mannheim sporting goods store and started pole vaulting, thereby keeping the brass at bay and not having to do side straddle hops. Above, old Mangan is about to break a perfectly good bamboo cross bar.

Tropical Diseases, Use of the Jungle Kit, and other mindless titles. We wondered why they were teaching us these things but we knew the ulterior motivation. You people are all going to the South Pacific. But I really thought, as did most of the squadron, "Give me thirty days in the States and you can ship my ass anywhere. Just don't get me killed."

The weather had been quite decent as June rolled around, perfect for pole vaulting. Then the rains came—as they did most of the time in Europe. The rain fell relentlessly for days on end. Meanwhile, trains ran day and night near the front of our house. GIs ran the trains, their engines pulling cars of every description. The cargo was unbelievable. About half of a train would be big long hospital cars marked with red crosses. They were still bringing wounded back from field hospitals. The rest of the train would be made up of open flat cars and coal cars filled with people, whole families. They were French, Polish, Hungarian, displaced persons from every country in Europe—soaked to the skin. Not a pretty sight. This was one war in which civilians took a real beating. Not only were most of the German cities either in ruins or obliterated, you would see hundreds of people with arms and legs gone, or worse.

Mid-summer weather around Mannheim was pleasantly warm after the rains stopped. So we spent a lot of our idle time outside the houses throwing softballs and watching the kids play. There was one bunch of little girls who didn't hate us at all, even though we were probably living in some of their houses. Their ages ranged from about seven to ten and they shouted and danced and all wanted chocolate bars and Lifesavers, which we finally had in abundance. Their ringleader was a ten-year-old kid named Trudy, a little golden blond with pigtails. I've always thought she would grow up to be Miss Germany—she was that cute. My buddies and I had a lot of fun trying to teach them English, and they were fast learners. They showed absolutely no fear of us, and I figured it was partly because the average American looked pretty much like the average German. And even better, GIs tended to be brash and fun loving. I couldn't help but wonder again how little kids like this could have had anything to do with Nazis. I doubt that they did. Of course, the war had just ended and that made a difference.

25

Going Home. Auf Wiedersehen Deutschland

By THE LAST WEEK in June 1945 the 10th and the other two squadrons in the 50th Group transferred our planes to the Army of Occupation in Mannheim. I didn't know how the pilots felt about giving away their own personal P-47s but most of us were glad to see them go since this became another mile on the road home. However, there had to be some nostalgia involved in getting rid of those magnificent flying machines. More than 15,000 P-47s had been produced by war's end. Everybody figured it wouldn't be long now until we knew what was going to happen. Rumors were still flying about going to Marseilles on the Mediterranean, then heading directly to the Pacific. I did a lot of praying that trip wouldn't occur—not just then anyway. A lot of us felt like the end of the war in Europe (V-E-Day) was sufficient. Now we could go home and buy a white shirt and two-tone shoes. But no, there was still another war breathing heavily on us in the Pacific.

SHAEF (Supreme Headquarters Allied Expeditionary Force)

announced that men with the longest battle service were to be reassigned to occupation duty or sent home. Others were to go on to the Pacific. Eligibility for duty or discharge was based on a point system. This was determined by length of service, time overseas, decorations, parenthood and age. I was shy some fifteen points of the necessary eighty-five to go home on furlough. Then we got five more points for the Ardennes (Bulge) and another five for Central Europe, giving me a total of eighty; hopefully enough to get me home. I figured they wouldn't send me direct to the Pacific for a lousy five points. Within days we climbed into trucks, along with all our stuff, going God knows where.

All the Mannheim kids gathered to wave goodbye. Little Trudy shouted at me to be sure and write her a letter from America. She even handed me a scrap of paper with her address written on it, along with a baby picture and a little silver colored medallion. My buddies roared with glee and kept asking me, "Isn't that kid a little young for you, Mangan?" We unloaded the rest of our GI goodies on the whole pack of kids and rode off into the sunrise. I know damn well all the neighborhood parents were shouting and slapping their *lederhosen* with joy to see us go. Especially since they could move back into their homes, hoping not too much of their fine china would find its way to America.

Our convoy crossed the nearby Rhine on a new GI bridge and we unloaded several miles away at a railhead. There were all these boxcars and a few antique passenger cars waiting at a siding and our instructions were to climb aboard and don't bitch about it. Our reasoning was, "After all we've done for God, Country and Flag, and you bastards are shipping us in freight cars?" Their reasoning was, "Okay, if you want to hang around Germany and wait for the Golden State Limited, be our guest." End of subject.

I remembered years ago reading about World War I trains hauling the doughboys to the front lines. They were packed in the famous 40 and 8 boxcars. That meant forty men or eight horses. Unbelievably, we were going to travel in those same cars—about half of us anyway. Painted in white letters on each of these reddish brown GI Pullmans were the words HOMMES—40 CHEVAUX—8. Inside the cars you sat or slept on bales of hay. We're talking nostalgia here.

We headed due west, back to Metz in France and then on to Verdun, passing through other old WWI battlefields. Our destination was Reims. Nearby was a huge tent city called Camp New York, a redeployment center. It was now official that we were being shipped to the States for thirty-day furloughs. Thank you God.

Camp New York was a tent city to end all tent cities. My luck was still holding, as we were the first troops to be processed, the first of hundreds of thousands, I guess millions eventually. The date was June 24, 1945. *The Stars and Stripes* ran a major story on the goodies coming to Camp New York. Everything would be first class, like beer, Cokes, and big USO shows. We were too early to get the promised treats since the fabled amenities hadn't yet arrived. There was nothing to do except watch thousands of soldiers moving into thousands of tents. There was no beer, no Cokes, no shows, no nothing. But most guys didn't bitch because we were going home and Camp New York was one step closer to the U.S.A.

We turned in most of our field equipment and supplies here, things like carbines, ammunition, trench knives, shovels, pup tents, sleeping bags, long underwear, that kind of stuff. It was a relief to unload it because it seemed to get heavier and heavier to lug around. Most of the troops usually played poker day and night. Lots of us had some money in our pockets so it was easy come, easy go. I just sat around and watched because I didn't know how to play. But it was fascinating to watch because some of the stakes became huge. I saw one of my buddies, a corporal named Leroy Bundy from some little coal town in Pennsylvania, sit in the tent one night and win $14,000. I heard later that he bought a new home with his winnings. You could buy a pretty nice home for $14,000 in 1945.

German prisoners of war handled all of the shit details at Camp New York and they didn't seem to mind at all. Anything was better than dying for your country in a losing war. The Americans treated them according to the Geneva Convention so their lives weren't all that bad. I remember one day there were four husky Germans digging a six-foot hole for a latrine close to our tent. The MPs asked me if I would guard these guys and I didn't mind because life was getting pretty boring anyway. Since we had already turned in our weapons, the M.P.s handed me a loaded carbine and pointed out that I should shoot if these guys started to walk. "Don't let them out of your sight." No problem. I watched them dig in the soft earth for several hours and that proved to be boring too. I walked over to a nearby tent so I could watch the poker game as well as the Germans. In a few minutes I looked back towards the beautiful hole in the ground, and sure enough my prisoners were gone. Panic time. Before panicking completely I walked over to the hole, thinking they might be in there. No prisoners. Then I began walking briskly (and nervously) around the whole area. And soon there they were, starting on the next hole. Thank God. These Germans had a real unlike-American attitude; instead of one guy digging and three guys watching and smoking, the Germans all worked. Then when they finished the first hole, they just calmly walked over to the next designated spot and began digging another hole. Maybe these people were supermen after all.

On each return trip from deep inside Germany, American trucks and converted bombers brought back plane loads of liberated Allied prisoners. They were unloaded at several of these tent cities for rehabilitation and early transfer to their homelands. At one camp near Le Havre, called Camp Lucky Strike, there were more than 47,000 recovered American prisoners. Some of them had been prisoners since the early battles in Tunisia in 1942. So we really didn't have anything to complain about, when we figured those poor bastards had been in German prison camps longer than most of us had been in the army. So we all just sat around and talked about food. We fantasized about all kinds of food, mostly hamburgers and French fries, and steaks and chocolate cake and ice cream and even salad.

After about two weeks in our favorite tent city, we got the good news to move on, this time to Camp Twenty Grand at Le Havre (some redeployment centers were named after American cigarettes) on the French Channel Coast. This is where the Germans thought the Allied invasion would take place, since it was only twenty some miles across the Channel from England. Because of that, two of Hitler's elite armies didn't get to the Normandy beaches until it was too late. Le Havre was left bristling with guns and troops while the Allies came ashore in Normandy. Good thinking, Ike.

Twenty Grand looked like Camp New York, with the color khaki as far as the eye could see. After only three days here we boarded a Liberty Ship in the harbor at Le Havre and landed in Southampton, England. I felt like we were half way home, perhaps because England was my favorite place in the ETO. At least they spoke our language—well sort of.

Next stop was a British Army base named Camp Barton Stacy near the town of Winchester. The accommodations were splendid (as the Brits would say). Since we didn't have any duty to pull, my pals and I walked into town every night to see the non-action. There was a pub in all its polished mahogany splendor in the center of town so we hung out there. What I didn't know until much later was that right next door a thousand-year-old medieval building still housed the original Round Table where King Arthur and his knights also hung out. I still feel dumb for not going into that old building. But how was I to know? In America we would have marked it properly with big flashing neon signs and arrows pointing out the place. You know, civilized. Another landmark I missed seeing was Winchester Cathedral. I don't think the song had been written yet. But one thing I soon discovered was the Winchester swimming pool. It was right downtown, walking distance from camp. I bought a pair of swim trunks and went swimming every day, even though the sky was always threatening rain and the cold water made my lips blue in no time. Most days the customers were just a half dozen goose-bumped English kids and me. But any port in a storm.

After two pretty nice weeks in Winchester we pulled out and headed by rail for Glasgow, Scotland and the Firth of Forth where she was waiting for us—the *Queen Mary,* the icing on the cake. Instead of leaving from Southampton on the English Channel, the brass felt it was still too risky because of German mines. They didn't want to lose the *Queen Mary,* nor did we. We began loading one morning and set sail the next afternoon, a total of 16,000 of us. That's a whole division and more. It took that long to get all of us on board. One of the ship's officers rounded us up in groups and said he was sorry to tell us but in order to get home quickly (by squeezing more troops on each trip) a lot of us wouldn't get to sleep inside the ship. We would have to sleep on deck and stay outside most of the time. A very surprised officer heard this mighty groundswell of pure joy erupting from the 50th Fighter Group and many others. I could hardly believe our good fortune, since you may recall the trauma of an earlier voyage on the *Stirling Castle* across the North Atlantic. This was wonderful, just breathing in the cool sea air. We each staked out a spot and it became a territorial thing. They issued us a blanket, and as soon as it got dark I crawled on top of it and slept like a baby. Naturally everybody slept in their clothes. That big old ship just cruised along at top speed, no U-boats to worry about this trip. The ocean

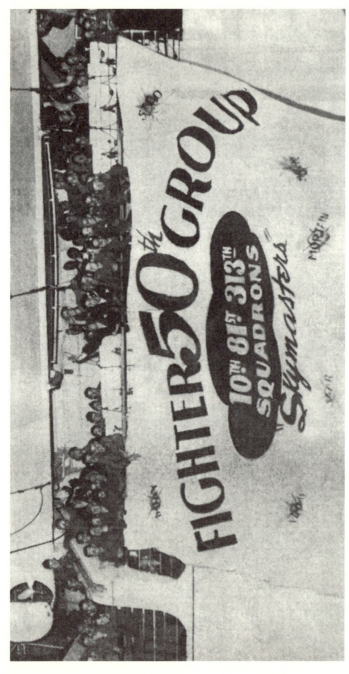

This photo appeared in a New York newspaper the day we arrived from Europe. The caption read, "Men who helped bring Nazis to their knees, cheer sight of New York from deck of peacetime luxury liner Queen Mary. Below them hangs banner of 50th Fighter Group, one of many flags denoting outfits of returning men, on sides of big ship."

was smooth as a lake and I didn't get seasick. I'm sure the time of year (the last of August) had a lot to do with my well-being.

Handsome mahogany rails about a foot wide stretched all around the edge of each deck. They were carved with the names of countless GIs. So I felt an obligation to carve my own as well—and did. After only four days at sea (compared to fifteen days going over) we saw the skyline of New York and looming dead ahead was the Statue of Liberty—looking like she was welcoming us home. "Give me your tired, your poor, your huddled masses...." I felt like we would qualify on each of these statements. I never realized it until that moment, but the Statue of Liberty was green. I always thought it would be silver or whitish in color. But all of this was indescribable. I'd seen a thousand movies in which immigrants were arriving in America and tearing up upon seeing first hand the Statue of Liberty, but I never thought I'd be lucky enough to see it this way.

Shortly we pulled in to a pier, the soldiers on the decks cheering at the throngs of people on the pier who waved American flags. A military band played John Phillips Souza marches and the whole scene was like a movie. The only thing missing was Jimmy Cagney singing and dancing "Yankee Doodle Dandy." Somebody draped a fifty-foot banner over the side of the ship which read 50th FIGHTER GROUP 10th 81st 313th SQUADRONS. And the names of all the places we had been were also painted on the banner. Next day the *New York Times* printed a four-column picture showing America's happy warriors arriving and there we were in the picture. Those were the great days when Americans really appreciated their military. Hell of a feeling.

26

Back on the Home Front

AFTER THAT HEADY WELCOME at Pier 90 in New York we boarded a troop train and chugged to nearby Camp Kilmer, New Jersey. Not to get choked up here, but just to stand on firm American soil at last was a beautiful feeling. Some of these guys literally kissed the ground. But then they were from New Jersey.

At Camp Kilmer we lined up alongside the train and the first voice we heard was that of a master sergeant whose voice boomed out, "Any of y'all got scabies?

One of our returning GIs boomed back, "What in the hell are scabies?

"I'll tell you what they are," the sergeant said. "They are little bitty bugs. You can't see 'em cause they burrow under your skin and lay their eggs and they're contagious as hell. They feed on cattle and sheep and even people. They cause ugly red scabs on your skin and they itch all the time. Does any of this sound familiar? Sure it does. I know where you people picked 'em up. Has anybody here been sleeping in German feather beds?"

Nobody breathed or made a move even though most of us had

been sleeping in German houses. Now I knew where I picked up all these scabs. I've got SCABIES. I figured if we told him our previous sleeping arrangements they might keep us here at Camp Kilmer till we got cured. This place was beginning to have Ellis Island written all over it. But this sergeant was not a bad sort. He'd been processing GIs returning from Europe and you could tell he had some respect for us, especially since he obviously sat out the war in Camp Kilmer. I knew none of us would raise a hand against him, but he didn't know that.

The trick now was to look cured and get out of there as soon as possible. This ploy took care of itself, however, when they ushered us in groups of about twenty to the Mother of all Shower Rooms. Other soldiers were already "cured" it seemed, since they walked out on their own two feet looking clean and shiny. The way it worked was we all stripped down and stepped under these very hot showers. Everybody's skin was the whitest of white— mine included, since the European climate hadn't been conducive to getting a suntan. They handed me an amber colored bar of GI soap that weighed at least a pound and was the strongest I ever put on my delicate body. They also handed me a scrub brush to help get that damn soap down under my skin. In seconds my skin was bright red from the lye in the soap, the bristle brush and the steaming hot water. Then came the *coup de grace.* They turned hoses on us that sprayed a milky-like substance that I later heard was DDT, the newest bug killer in the world.

But the worst was over. We turned in our clothes for freshly washed uniforms, shorts, T-shirts and all. Before we settled in for the night we were directed to a brightly lit mess hall. They fed us huge T-bone steaks, baked potatoes, fresh fruit, apple pie (really) and everything we'd been missing for several years. It was a splendid feast, served on aluminum trays—not a mess kit in sight. The taste of that food was indescribable, right out of a recruitment poster.

Next day I passed a cursory inspection and they pronounced me cured of my dread disease. I signed several pieces of paper in exchange for some chits for meals, walking around money, and best of all a train ticket to Fort Bliss, where I arrived three days later to begin my thirty-day furlough. My family had moved into a new house while I'd been gone. Home was now only about a mile and a half from Fort Bliss, but I felt like the army owed me a taxi ride home after all I'd done for them.

It was the fifth of August '45, one of those El Paso days I'd been dreaming about. As the cab stopped in front of a house I had never seen, my mother came running out to the curb to hug her long lost son, checking to see if I was still all in one piece. My sister Romaine and brother Billy brought up the rear. They had each grown a foot. I guess the abrazos were similar in other war-time homecomings but they couldn't have been greater than this one. And others' chocolate cake couldn't compare. When we got all the family and extended family together, somebody asked me to tell them about the war. Then somebody else said, "Oh no, I'm sure Frank doesn't want to talk about it." I just smiled and ate another piece of chocolate cake.

It was like a dream being home again. The sunshine was out-standing. My morale zoomed off the charts. I tried not to think about the future and the Pacific—not dwelling on it but I couldn't help realizing the war was only half over. I didn't have a clue then but plans were already formed. The Allies planned to invade the Japanese home island of Kyusu in November of '45, little more than two months away. This was to be followed in March '46 with the assault on Honshu, the main home island. And it was bound to be sheer murder.

But the Mangan luck was still intact. Unknown to me and most of the world, America had exploded the first atomic bomb in the New Mexico desert near Alamogordo on July 16. People in El Paso reported seeing the pre-dawn sky light up, but the military announced only that a large ammunition dump had exploded. Most people shrugged and bought the story. The day after I got home, on August 6, an American B-29 named Enola Gay dropped an atomic bomb on Hiroshima. The city was incinerated. The bomb made an invasion of Japan unnecessary. Three days later America dropped a second atomic bomb on Nagasaki and that was the end of the war, just like that. Japan quit and signed the terms of surrender on September 2. Thank you Harry Truman.

For me, the timing couldn't have been better. Here I was at home in the lap of luxury, eating Mom's apple pie, sleeping in my own bed in my own room and the stinking war ends. What happens now? A look at my orders told me that my thirty days would be up the fifth of September and I was to turn myself in at La Junta Army Airfield in Colorado. I could do that easily, especially since this whole mess was over over there. At least I was going to have some fun at home. I got a date with a very cute girl from high school days named Anna Jo Davis. I realized I still had some scabies, but you can't cut yourself off from civilization. We went downtown and took in a movie at the Plaza Theater. I was no longer getting in free like the pre-war days when I ushered there or had buddies there taking tickets. But after all I was a serviceman in uniform and they gave us a half price rate, which I think was twenty-five cents in 1945. The interior of that theater was beautiful and there was romance in the air. Until I felt the first signs of my unwelcome bugs, the return of the mange. I had finally gotten rid of most of them from all over my body but some of the little bastards just wouldn't let go. By this time you can guess where they were—in a very embarrassing place. Maybe it was the cool air conditioning, but I itched like crazy and I was afraid to scratch. So after the show I took that pretty American girl to the Oasis Drive-in for one coke and then quickly drove her home.

27

The End of the Line

IT WAS EARLY SEPTEMBER when I checked in at La Junta Army Airfield in Colorado. A light snow on the ground told me that it was already winter up there, and naturally I happened to be wearing a summer cotton uniform. A sergeant pointed me in the direction of some tarpaper barracks where the rest of the 10th was settling in. Even though it had only been a month since I'd been around these foxhole buddies, it was good seeing them and listening to their lies about their numerous dates and conquests back home. All those muddy months in France and Germany had formed a bond between us that you seldom feel in civilian life. I was the only one who still had scabies while on furlough. Naturally, they thought that was funny as hell.

At La Junta the 50th Fighter Group was getting ready to go overseas and we were delighted to find out that the 50th now had 100 percent replacements. All the old boys like me had been replaced with Second Air Force recruits. Since the 50th was originally a peacetime outfit it wasn't deactivated like most other wartime units. So we just sat around and smoked cigarettes and enjoyed watching these new guys train and get ready to go overseas. Much of the 10th had already been mustered out, since they had the necessary magic points—like years in the service. The rest of us were still sweating it out.

La Junta wasn't much of an army town. Too many troops and nothing to do. I guess it would have been okay without all the soldiers standing around on every street corner watching the traffic lights change from red to green. All of my buddies from back east had been looking forward to Colorado, figuring that since they had to go back to the army anyway, it might as well be a decent place. They had visions of snow-capped mountains, pine and fir forests like Austria, and clear cold mountain streams, only to discover this wasn't that part of Colorado. It was definitely not the Rocky Mountains. Especially around La Junta. The town was situated out on the bald prairie where on a clear day you could see half way across central Kansas. This was an extension of the Great Plains where they still grow all that wheat. C'est la guerre.

There were five hundred of us Ninth Air Force guys at La Junta. All of us had over eighty points, the new magic number that was good for a discharge. These feather merchants and their fellow drones of the Second Air Force were supposed to be processing us for speedy discharge. Time hung heavy as hell for us and nothing was happening. We appointed a tech sergeant to pay a visit to the nearest orderly room and find out what was causing the slowdown. A Second Air Force captain agreed to see our sergeant since he represented some five hundred men struggling to get out of there. The captain informed him that they didn't have, as he put it, "sufficient personal" to process us. The trouble was, they didn't work. They didn't work Saturdays or Sundays, they took off Wednesday afternoons. They took two hours for lunch and an hour for coffee breaks twice a day. What pissed us off was that for the last year and a half we kept moving twenty-four hours a day, seven days a week and didn't take coke breaks at a non-existent corner drug store. We all got the captain's message which caused fights and near-fights every day.

If we hadn't been so close to getting out of La Junta, the next skirmish might have turned into a mutiny. It was caused by what became known as the Eisenhower Jacket Affair. The original story goes that General Eisenhower noticed the short, waist-length British battle jackets (which were decent looking) and decided to design one for himself. It created a lot of press that spread quickly among American troops under Eisenhower in Europe. The general ordered that American troops under his command would now be issued the new short jacket and would turn in their regulation long blouses. The troops mostly felt that the Ike Jacket was about the only thing the army ever issued that was half way presentable. It probably sounds kind of silly and meaningless nowadays, but we felt a little distinction wearing them. Maybe it was because the GIs in the States weren't allowed to.

At any rate, one morning an order came through signed by the base commander that all Eisenhower jackets were to be turned in to Supply immediately and that we would draw the regulation blouse. What was left of the 50th Fighter Group went nuts. Somehow the word got out quickly and within two days the commander was ordered to rescind his (really) stupid decision. Which he did. The final insult was that we were then informed that seventy of our service records had been lost and that we would be in La Junta indefinitely until the records were found, perhaps two more months.

Following the latest debacle, I felt like I had to get out of there —even for a few days. My sister, Mary Lou, was in school at the University of Colorado in Boulder. So I managed a three-day pass, and complete with Eisenhower jacket, took off toward Boulder via Denver. I boarded a Greyhound bus in La Junta at noon on a Friday and had to stand up all the way to Pueblo.

Considering the throngs of people at every bus and train depot I figured I was lucky to just get on the bus. Standing in the aisle was easy—until we reached about half way between Colorado Springs and Denver. That's when the bus broke down.

Most of my fellow passengers sat there and waited for something to happen. Some of us got out of the bus and sat on the side of the road and watched the driver work on the engine. At least I got to sit down, but after watching the driver tinkering around for two hours I knew he was over his head. I took my musette bag off the bus, thanked the poor driver for the ride thus far and started thumbing. An hour later I rode into Denver with a high school football team on a yellow school bus. It was one noisy, wild ride.

In Denver I rushed over to Greyhound only to find out I'd missed the Boulder bus by three minutes. It was 9:00 P.M. then. The next bus was scheduled to leave at 1:00 A.M. So after trying a thousand hotels in vain, I decided to wait for the next bus. I was sitting in the bus station with the usual rumpled crew. Slumped over next to me was a passed-out soldier, holding on to a full bottle of Calverts Reserve. The bottle slipped out of his hands, splashed all over me and started running on the floor. With a lightning maneuver I scooped up the bottle and saved three-fourths of it for him, then put the bottle behind us on a shelf.

About that time a scungy-looking civilian started eyeing the elusive bottle. He produced a brown paper sack, leaned over me and proceeded to put the bottle in it and walk off. This guy was a tub of lard and was accompanied by a skinny pal. Together they reminded me of Laurel and Hardy

So I said, "Hey, put the bottle back."

"Who are you, this guy's guardian?" said the big man.

I said, "I don't like to see you roll a drunk, especially a soldier."

Well, by this time everybody in the bus station started crowding around listening to us arguing and hoping to see a fight. A sailor said, "Deck him soldier." So with that, my chubby opponent took off his glasses, handed them to his friend and said to me, "Lets go for a walk."

.That suited me fine. We went outside and walked half a block with about fifty people following. He said, "You goddamn soldiers all think just because you got a uniform on you can tell the rest of us what to do." He quickly followed that remark with a looping right meant for my chin. He missed by a mile and as he leaned into me I got lucky with a very short punch that landed in his middle immediately below the rib cage. He just gasped, sunk to his knees, rolled over groaning and became deathly quiet. End of fight. I didn't want to kill the bastard; I just wanted to maim him.

Just then the MPs arrived and said to me, "What's the trouble sergeant?" I didn't have to explain as the crowd did that for me. One MP pulled my recent opponent to his feet and told him and his buddy to get out of there before there was any more trouble. And that was it. So I lit a cigarette, feeling a lot like Humphrey Bogart and climbed on the bus for Boulder.

We got to Boulder at 2:30 A.M. and naturally the way my luck had been running, all hotels were full. I thought about calling my sister for advice, but since she lived in the Kappa house and it was now 3:00 A.M. I decided to try rooming houses. After walking around in the dark awhile, I spotted a handsome old Victorian looking two-story house that had a light on. I woke up the owner and she told me she was full up but I could sleep on the floor for $1.50. This old girl must have been getting rich, because there were servicemen almost wall to wall asleep on the floors.

That was okay with me although not as comfortable as a German feather bed. I folded my jacket for a pillow, stripped down to my shorts, put my wallet under the jacket and went right to sleep. Within minutes I felt somebody's hand groping for my wallet. I thought, "Here we go again, only this time I'm getting rolled." So I said loudly, "What's the trouble?" And you know what he said? "Say, have you got a match?" And at 3:30 in the morning, yet.

I overslept but I remember waking up on that lady's parlor floor. I looked around and saw that all the other guests had departed and three gray haired ladies were sitting on the sofa reading Sunday's *Denver Post*. They didn't seem perturbed to have a soldier sleeping on a bare floor in his shorts. Nothing's too good for our servicemen.

Anyway, I survived the night and spent a fine day with my sister roaming around the campus and catching up with each other's lives. Then, I had to get back to camp. So I caught the 6:00 P.M. bus to Denver. I had a layover until 12:30 A.M. so I took in a show and supper. My bus finally arrived and got to Pueblo at 4:00 A.M. I got off the bus and had a cup of lousy coffee. When I started to reboard at 4:30, the driver informed four of us GIs that the bus was already loaded to capacity. Big mistake getting off for that coffee. The driver said that we could wait for the next bus, which left at noon. This was not the time in my career to make trouble, but by now I really began to hate civilians.

So the four of us got out on the highway and started sweating out rides. It was pitch dark and plenty cold. Exactly two cars came by in the next three hours. Finally a GI drove by about 8:00 A.M. and took us all the way to La Junta. And I thought life in the European Theater of Operations was rough.

When I rejoined my buddies at the base they were full of rumors that the we were on the verge of leaving La Junta. Later I discovered that out of five hundred guys in the 50th Group, I was one of twenty lucky GIs to be placed on shipment orders, slated to go to Tucson for separation. Rather strange I thought since they could just as easily have sent me to Bliss and I could have walked home. But I don't take no stinking chances. Like all good soldiers I kept my mouth shut for once, knowing that in a couple of days these people at La Junta would turn me loose. There was one last thing I'd been wondering about and that was my like-new Speed Graphic.

You see, after the Germans quit we were still in Mannheim. So we packed all the squadron equipment and sent it to La Junta Air Force Base for later shipment to the Pacific. I had packed the Speed Graphic along with other photo stuff in Mannheim. All of this was now carefully stored on a taxi strip covered with tarps. I reasoned that with no war on now, what on earth did the army need with another camera? So in the dark of night I lifted up the tarp, pried open the crate marked 10th Photo and guess what was missing? The camera, of course. That fighter pilot George Johnson had beat me to it.

Funny thing happened. In 1946 I entered the University of Missouri at Columbia and the first guy I ran into was my friend George Johnson, the intrepid fighter pilot. When I accused him of larceny and theft from the United States Government—and me, he just smiled and said, "Rank hath its privileges, old man, it was a dirty war." There in Columbia, Johnson was with his new bride who was easily pretty enough to be Most Beautiful Girl on campus. For that reason only I didn't press charges.

About the time I got over *l'affaire Speed Graphic*, I did indeed get my orders to proceed to Davis Monthan Air Field in Tucson. For a change it was an easy and uneventful bus ride; I almost missed the usual hassle and stress. In Tucson I found a nearly empty barracks in which I bunked. Late the next afternoon after swearing that I was of sound mind and body and with my discharge safely in hand, they gave me a gold-colored lapel pin that proclaimed I was officially mustered out. As I recall the pin was a gold eagle, but everybody called it the Ruptured Duck.

For some reason I never forgot that last afternoon. It was partly because the early November twilight cast a gloomy shadow over the empty barracks. Everything was dead quiet. Right then it seemed as if this whole bloody war had died with a whimper. I guess this is the way a war ends. But that's just my opinion.

I picked up my barracks bag and started walking out the door. A real nice kid sitting on an empty cot said, "So long, Sarg, see you in the next war."

Afterword

HOW DOES ONE BECOME a civilian again? When I got home in November 1945 I expected to face major culture shock on the move back into my hometown. But no, I was able to put wartime on hold and focus on peacetime, getting a decent job or going back to college and the sooner the better. I couldn't block out the war years, but I just wanted to get back to the real world. I think Americans in general felt pretty much the same way. People didn't even ask me about, say, the Battle of the Bulge (probably because they had never heard of it) so I had no reason to bore them with the details. Life was delicious.

It was too late to get into a college for the 1945 fall semester. So I put higher education on hold and found a job at Don Thompson's Sporting Goods store. With my mustering out pay I bought a pin-stripe suit, white shirt and a pair of two-tone shoes. Less than a week after becoming a card-carrying civilian, I was working eight to five and riding the Government Hill bus to work.

Mr. Thompson was another one of those wonderful misguided

souls who heard that Mangan was this talented artist who had just returned from overseas where he painted pin-up girls on airplane cowlings all over Western Europe. Since this heady reputation preceded me, who was I to deny it and probably ruin my image? So Mr. Thompson put me to work as the store's window trimmer. I didn't have the foggiest idea about how to decorate store windows with eye-catching displays. So I bought a bunch of colored crepe paper and muddled through the first day by attaching footballs and other sports stuff to colored streamers. I started to ask the boss what he thought of the idea of me painting a couple of Mexicans wearing big sombreros leaning against a tall saguaro cactus (my main claim to fame). And since much of the store's income came from the sale of guns and ammunition, we could display real pistols and rifles alongside my revolutionaries. I could tell this idea would go nowhere, especially since Mr. Thompson really liked my crepe paper theme. But 1945 was a good year.

Mr. Thompson did, however, put me in the firearms department assisting a Mexican-American cowboy named Juan Escontrias. Juan always carried a revolver on his hip. I first thought it was to attract attention to the gun department. But no, it was for something more important, like self-defense. Turns out old Juan went across the Rio Grande to Juarez one night where he shot and killed a powerful Mexican army colonel. After that Juan always packed a gun. I didn't think it was legal in Texas in those days, but nobody ever messed with Juan Escontrias. He was a very macho guy, though he never returned to Juarez. One day he showed me his .45 revolver and I told him I'd been carrying a loaded carbine myself for the best part of two years. Juan brightened up and became real interested. He would have loved that war and been a hell of a soldier (if he was on our side) but he was way over the age limit. He told me his family owned Hueco Tanks which is now a Texas state park about twenty miles east of El Paso.

I picked up a few merchandizing secrets from old Juan, as well as from Mr. Thompson himself during my tenure at his store. A few days before Christmas business was not all that great. We had a year's supply of men's leather wallets. The price tag was $5.00 and I thought they would be nice gifts for women to purchase for their husbands or boyfriends. However, the wallets just sat there, nobody buying. So I told the boss my problem. He smiled and said, "Change all the price tags to $10.00."

While I was reluctantly doubling the price tags, women began to stop and admire my wallets. Then they began buying them as fast as I raised the prices. By Christmas Eve we were out of leather wallets. It didn't take me long to realize that women actually liked the wallets, but they felt that $5.00 for a gift wasn't nice or expensive enough.

Meanwhile, I really wanted to get into the advertising business and get out of waiting on customers. The truth is, waiting on customers was a lot more fun than freezing my butt off in some Frenchman's apple orchard but I wanted something better. So I crossed the street for an appointment with Dan White, one of two advertising heads in El Paso. His agency had about fifteen employees, and I told him that I'd like to be one of them. "My experience? Well actually, uhh, none."

"We do need to fill a vacancy in the art and production department," said Mr. White. "But we're looking for somebody who can go to work today. My advice for you if you want into advertising is to find a good art or design or creative writing school."

I knew Dan was right so I aimed for the University of Missouri School of Journalism. There was one hitch. They informed me I didn't have the right credentials to be accepted. Before the war I spent two years at Texas College of Mines (now the University of Texas at El Paso). I was sixteen when I first entered and soon discovered I was way over my head trying to understand classics like *Beowulf* in the original Old English. I wasted an inordinate amount of time in English 101 carving my initials into the ancient college desktops.

In 1946 I reentered the College of Mines and this time around I moved briskly through those once-unattainable grades. Going back to college was, for me, the smoothest way to slide back into civilian life and not dwell on wartime events. Occasionally, though, past experiences popped up. It had been only about six months since the war in Europe ended and I was still jumpy at the least little noise. One afternoon I was sitting in a Government class on the top floor of what was known as Old Main. Professor Gladys Gregory was droning on about fascism. I figured I already knew about facism. I was nodding off, as were about twenty other ex-GIs in the classroom of about a hundred students. Just then, I came fully awake hearing the loudest BOOM since Germany. It was like a violent explosion on the roof right over our heads. After having experienced similar sounds for the last several years I automatically hit the floor and flattened out, glancing around for someplace to hide. I looked under the desks and saw the other vets trying to dig holes in the concrete floor. Then we all realized at once the ear-shattering sound was obviously caused by a very large military airplane buzzing Old Main, probably to impress the pilot's girlfriend. At this juncture the ex-soldiers began struggling up into their seats and all had kind of sheepish looks. We were embarrassed until our professor smiled and said, "That's all right, gentlemen. You've just given me a true story to tell my grandchildren some day."

That summer, 1946, another explosion caused my instant reaction. The City was happy to rehire me as a lifeguard at Memorial Pool. It was the Fourth of July and I was sitting atop the guard stand when a carload of teenage boys drove up outside our chair link fence. One kid lobbed a cherry bomb over the fence. It exploded just as it hit the water under me and damn near hit a little girl in the face. In about one second I was off the stand and running toward the entrance gate. Once outside I picked up a round rock about the size of baseball. The boys figured retreat was the better part of valor, so they gunned their car and peeled out of the parking area. They were only about twenty yards away when I heaved my missile. I figured it was about a hundred-to-one chance of hitting the target. But that beautiful rock hit the car's rear window dead center and crashed inside, splintering everybody with shattered glass. The pool customers cheered. It was a lovely day.

The University of Missouri finally accepted my college grades, and off I went to a new experience. The campus seemed huge to me, but it was teeming with returning GIs so I never felt like a lost soul. I even joined a fraternity.

Two years later, back in El Paso, and clutching a sheepskin that said Mangan was now a Bachelor of Journalism, I made another appointment with Dan White of the advertising agency. I told him, without my earlier humility, of my new wealth of knowledge and vast experience working on *The Columbia Missourian*, a daily newspaper. "Well Mr. White, I'm ready to go right to work. Today."

"Well, Pancho, (he remembers me enough to call me Pancho) the person we're looking for is somebody with no pre-conceived knowledge of this business. I need a person who I can mold into our firm's creative system, that is, with an open mind uncluttered with old ideas. I'm sure you understand our position."

Two words came out of my mouth, "Holy Jesus."

When I regained a little composure, I said, "Dan, (I now called him Dan) don't you remember me? I'm the guy you advised to get an education. I just graduated from the nation's first school of journalism and I'm here to go to work."

Mr. White slumped lower in his leather chair, and with a sly grin, he said, "Yeah, I remember telling you that, Pancho, and by god you're right. When can you start to work?"

Well, I started to work the next day and the agency proved

a pleasant choice. At first I had zero confidence in my total immersion into writing ad copy and doing simple artwork but it turned out okay and I've been doing similar work ever since.

Now, about the French girls: they both corresponded with me off and on for forty years. Both actually made trips to America. Monique La Fay married a nice guy who owned a ski shop in the French Alps. In 1980 they visited my wife Judy and me in El Paso. Their son, a teenager named JonLuc visited us twice, once with his girlfriend. The first day they showed up the temperature was 112 degrees (new record for El Paso). JonLuc said he wanted to go where it was *really* hot, so we poured them on Greyhound for Death Valley. Another time, I got a phone call from Simone LaCroix. She was in Clovis, New Mexico trying to track down an American GI boyfriend at Clovis Air Force Base. He was serving with, unbelievably, my old outfit the 10th Fighter Squadron. I was no help.

In the interim, the squadron remained active, flying out of Hahn Airbase in West Germany for thirty-two years. During the Gulf War it flew F-16 fighters. In 1994 it's name changed to the 10th Flight Test Squadron located at Tinker Air Force Base, Oklahoma.

For at least four decades following the war, there was relatively little in print or in documentaries about World War II compared to what we see today. It took years for Americans to get a proper perspective. Those of us who lived it feel complimented by the attention and most are in agreement that new generations should understand what happened to the world back in the 1940s. People still can't imagine what any part of World War II was like. You had to be there.

It was a long way from Texas to Central Europe and back again. And after four birthdays in uniform, life for me would never be the same. In many ways it would be better, but it would never be quite the same. Thinking back, it had been a long stretch from those idyllic years before the war as a happy teenager; from lazy sunburned summers lifeguarding at the city pools and winters ushering at the elegant Plaza Theater. It was a magical time.

Never such innocence again.

Acknowledgments

INITIALLY, my intent in writing this book was to record for close family members a brief description of personal adventures and travels in Europe during World War II, from 1942 to 1945. As I got into the project, however, a larger picture began to emerge. My wife, Judy, and my children, Peggy and Pancho, could not have been more supportive and loving. They suggested (no, insisted) that I expand my notes and letters into a book. It became a personal narrative that followed part of the course of wartime Europe—as accurately as I could recall.

I was able to track my squadron's whereabouts much of the time, but most dates and troop movements were obtained from army buddies who kept excellent notes. My sincere thanks to Harry Kaiser from Cincinnati, Ohio for corresponding with me all these years, and for remembering when and where so many events happened. Thanks also to Phil Pearce, foxhole buddy from Prospect, Kentucky who took some of the photos in this book. I'm indebted to Bernie Morrison from Fayetteville, Georgia for continuing to publish the *10th Fighter Squadron Newsletter* and keeping us all in touch.

Special thanks to author-historian Leon Metz of El Paso for reading the manuscript and giving me his always valuable suggestions and support. Lieutenant Colonel Kenny Wilkerson, Tinker Air Force Base, Oklahoma provided valuable early history of the 50th Fighter Group. Thanks to long-time friend Mandy Zabriskie from Indianapolis, Indiana for his copy editing, confidence and editorial know-how.

Finally, my deep appreciation goes to Sandy Schwarz of New York, New York who once wrote a fascinating essay on Zephyrhills, Florida—and included it in his memoir *War Is Hell, but Not All the Time*. I gleaned so much from Sandy's humanity and wonderful sense of humor.

Sources

The Rise and Fall of the Third Reich by William Shirer, *The Brass Ring* by Bill Mauldin, *Crusade in Europe* by Dwight D. Eisenhower, *My War* by Andy Rooney, *World War II*, Time-Life Books, *The Ninth Air Force in World War II* by Ken Rust, *Legacy, the Impact of World War II* by Barthy Bird, University of Texas at El Paso, *The Other Side of Time* by Brenden Phibbs, *Report by the Supreme Commander to the Combined Chiefs of Staff in Europe of the Allied Expeditionary Force* by Dwight D. Eisenhower.

Index

THIS BOOK

was printed on 60-pound Glatfelter Supple Opague Recycled Natural, an acid-free paper having an effective life of at least three hundred years. Text was set in New Caledonia. Chapter heads were set in Times New Roman. Title type is Stencil. Printing/ binding is by Thomson-Shore, Dexter, Michigan. Design: Vicki Trego Hill and Frank Mangan.